A Brave New Series

GLOBAL ISSUES
IN A CHANGING WORLD

This new series of short, accessible think pieces deals with leading global issues of relevance to humanity today. Intended for the enquiring reader and social activists in the North and the South, as well as students, the books explain what is at stake and question conventional ideas and policies. Drawn from many different parts of the world, the series' authors pay particular attention to the needs and interests of ordinary people, whether living in the rich industrial or the developing countries. They all share a common objective: to help stimulate new thinking and social action in the opening years of the new century.

Global Issues in a Changing World is a joint initiative by Zed Books in collaboration with a number of partner publishers and non-governmental organizations around the world. By working together, we intend to maximize the relevance and availability of the books published in the series.

PARTICIPATING NGOS

- *Both ENDS, Amsterdam*
- *Catholic Institute for International Relations, London*
- *Corner House, Sturminster Newton*
- *Focus on the Global South, Bangkok*
- *Inter Pares, Ottawa*
- *Third World Network, Penang*
- *World Development Movement, London*

*

'Communities in the South are facing great difficulties in coping with global trends. I hope this brave new series will throw much needed light on the issues ahead and help us choose the right options.'
Martin Khor, Director, Third World Network

'There is no more important campaign than our struggle to bring the global economy under democratic control. But the issues are fearsomely complex. This Global Issues Series is a valuable resource for the committed campaigner and the educated citizen.'
Barry Coates, Director, World Development Movement (WDM)

Titles in the Global Issues Series

For full details of this list and Zed's other subject and general
catalogues, please write to: The Marketing Department, Zed Books, 7 Cynthia Street,
London N1 9JF, UK or email Sales@zedbooks.demon.co.uk

Visit our website at: http:/www.zedbooks.demon.co.uk

ABOUT THIS BOOK

'John Madeley's book is a timely and important resource for the growing debate on trade and agriculture and the review of the WTO rules that promote trade at the cost of livelihood and food security. John combines the perspectives of people in the South and North to create another agenda for food based on justice and human rights. This book is an important milestone on the road towards food democracy.'

– *Vandana Shiva*

'A comprehensive and critical look at the impact of trade policy on food security in the South. John Madeley's impressive book offers a unique overview of how new trade rules governing intellectual property rights and agriculture have damaged the sector most vital to developing countries' future.'

– *Sophia Murphy, Senior Associate, Institute for Agriculture and Trade Policy*

For years, rich and poor citizens have been told that so-called free trade is the answer to their food needs. John Madeley's book is a marvellous riposte to this view. It explains why millions of people are questioning the neo-liberal trade pact and demanding a re-think.'

– *Tim Lang, Professor of Food Policy, Thames Valley University*

'This timely book is a welcome contribution to the disentangling of two vital global issues: poverty and trade. It is essential reading for anyone concerned with how we might evolve a more sustainable and equitable world.'

– *Professor Jules Pretty, Centre for Environment and Society, University of Essex*

'This book presents a powerful challenge to current free trade orthodoxy and it is essential reading, and not just for WTO students and campaigners. John Madeley has spent his life advocating the cause of farmers in the poorer countries and he knows they are still victims of our wealth and our greed. We are all involved in trade, whether we come in the disguise of consumers, aid workers, executives, negotiators or diplomats. His ability to research complex issues like TRIPS, genetically modified foods and the CAP, and to explain in simple terms how they are damaging the poor, is astounding. And we know he is right.'

– *John Montagu, Earl of Sandwich*

ABOUT THE AUTHOR

John Madeley has been a writer and broadcaster specializing in Third World development and environmental issues for the past twenty years. From 1983 to 1998, he was the editor of *International Agricultural Development*. A contributor to newspapers such as the *Observer*, the *Financial Times* and the *Independent on Sunday*, he has also written for Christian Aid, the Panos Institute, the Catholic Institute for International Relations and other NGOs. He is the author of several books:

- *When Aid is No Help: How Projects Fail and How They Could Succeed*
- *Trade and the Poor: the Impact of International Trade on Developing Countries*
- *Land is Life: Land Reform and Sustainable Agriculture* (co-editor)
- *Big Business, Poor Peoples: the Impact of Transnational Corporations on the World's Poor.*

A GLOBAL ISSUES TITLE

HUNGRY
FOR
TRADE

How the Poor Pay for Free Trade

John Madeley

Zed Books
London and New York

Pluto Press
Australia

University Press Ltd
Dhaka

White Lotus Co. Ltd
Bangkok

Fernwood Publishing Ltd
Halifax, Nova Scotia

David Philip
Cape Town

Hungry for Trade: How the Poor Pay for Free Trade
was first published in 2000 by

In Australasia: Pluto Press Australia, 6A Nelson Street,
Annandale, NSW 2038, Sydney

In Bangladesh: The University Press Ltd, Red Crescent Building,
114 Motijheel C/A, PO Box 2611, Dhaka 1000

In Burma, Cambodia, Laos, Thailand and Vietnam:
White Lotus Co. Ltd, GPO Box 1141, Bangkok 10501, Thailand.

In Canada: Fernwood Publishing Ltd, PO Box 9409, Station A,
Halifax, Nova Scotia, Canada B3K 5S3

In Southern Africa: David Philip Publishers (Pty Ltd),
208 Werdmuller Centre, Claremont 7735, South Africa

In the rest of the world:
Zed Books Ltd., 7 Cynthia Street, London N1 9JF, UK and
Room 400, 175 Fifth Avenue, New York, NY 10010, USA

Distributed in the USA exclusively by St Martin's Press, Inc.,
175 Fifth Avenue, New York, NY 10010, USA

Copyright © John Madeley 2000
Cover design by Andrew Corbett
Set in 10/13 pt Monotype Bembo by Long House, Cumbria, UK
Printed and bound in the United Kingdom by Cox & Wyman, Reading

A catalogue record for this book is available from the British Library
US CIP is available from the Library of Congress
Canadian CIP is available from the National Library of Canada

ISBN 1 86403 130 1 Pb (Australasia)
ISBN 1 55266 037 0 Pb (Canada)
ISBN 0 86486 367 5 Pb (Southern Africa)
ISBN 1 85649 864 6 Hb (Zed Books)
ISBN 1 85649 865 4 Pb (Zed Books)

CONTENTS

ACKNOWLEDGEMENTS

In writing an account as wide-ranging as this one I owe a debt of gratitude to many people for their insights and support. In particular I would like to thank Clive Robinson of Christian Aid and George Gelber of the Catholic Agency for Overseas Development (CAFOD), both of whom asked me to write material on trade and food security in 1999 and so focused my attention and research on these issues. My thanks are due to representatives of non-governmental organizations who have been at the forefront of exposing what really underlies trade and food issues, especially Walden Bello, Martin Khor, Devinder Sharma, Vandana Shiva, Antonio Tujan and other NGO workers who attended a consultation in the Netherlands in April 1999 about the effects of trade liberalization on the poor. And to the small farmers from developing countries who told me what trade liberalization has meant for them.

I would like especially to thank Claire Melamed of Christian Aid and Sophia Murphy of the Institute for Agriculture and Trade Policy who read drafts of this account and made some most helpful comments. And my sincere thanks to Alison for her diligent proof-reading and to Robert at Zed for his encouragement and enthusiasm. Any mistakes are entirely mine.

ABBREVIATIONS

ACP	African, Caribbean and Pacific countries
AIE	Analysis and information exchange
APRODEV	Association of World Council of Churches-related Development Organizations in Europe
ASEAN	Association of Southeast Asian Nations
CAFOD	Catholic Agency for Overseas Development
CAP	Common Agricultural Policy
CBD	(UN) Convention on Biodiversity
CGIAR	Consultative Group on International Agricultural Research
CIDSE	International Cooperation for Development and Solidarity
CIIR	Catholic Institute for International Relations
Conaprole	National Cooperative of Milk Producers (Uruguay)
ECA	Economic Commission for Africa
ESAP	Economic Structural Adjustment Programme
EU	European Union
FAO	Food and Agriculture Organization
FLO	FairTrade Labelling Organizations
GAO	Grupo de Agricultura Organica
GATT	General Agreement on Tariffs and Trade
GM	Genetically modified
GMB	Grain Marketing Board (Zimbabwe)
GMO	Genetically modified organism
GURT	Genetic use restriction technology

HIPC	Heavily Indebted Poor Countries (Debt Initiative)
ILO	International Labour Organization
IMF	International Monetary Fund
IPC	Integrated Programme for Commodities
IPM	Integrated pest management
LDCs	Least developed countries
MAI	Multilateral Agreement on Investment
NAFTA	North Atlantic Free Trade Agreement
NFIDC	Net-food-importing developing country
NGDO	Non-governmental development organization
NGDO-EU	Liaison Committee of Development NGOs to the European Union
NGO	Non-governmental organization
OAU	Organization of African Unity
PDHRE	People's Decade for Human Rights Education
RAFI	Rural Advancement Foundation International
SAARC	South Asian Association for Regional Cooperation
SADC	Southern African Development Community
SAP	Structural adjustment programme
TNC	Transnational corporation
TRIMs	Trade Related Investment Measures
TRIPs	Trade Related Intellectual Property Rights
UN	United Nations
UNCTAD	United Nations Conference on Trade and Development
UNDP	United Nations Development Programme
UNEP	United Nations Environment Programme
UPOV	Union for the Protection of New Varieties
US	United States
WFS	World Food Summit
WHO	World Health Organization
WTO	World Trade Organization
WWF–UK	World Wildlife Fund – United Kingdom

INTRODUCTION

'As long as I've eaten and filled the tummy,
what happens next I leave to God' –
African saying

The proverbial visitors from Mars to planet Earth might have some difficulty understanding the way that earthdwellers connect food and trade. Food is the most basic need of these people, they might reason, yet they have subordinated this to the rules and regulations of international trade. They have elevated trade into a kind of God; nothing must interfere with it, not even food. If a country wants to pass laws that enable it to feed its people, and those laws are not consistent with so called 'free' trade, they are disallowed. Trade is thus given a higher priority than food. The governments of planet Earth have boxed themselves into a corner, they may reason; their poor look for bread but are offered the stone of free trade.

Again the visitors may wonder why planet Earth is so divided, with a small number of rich countries but a much larger number of poor countries. They may scratch their heads at why countries that are poor, with so many hungry people, seem able to grow food quite abundantly on their land. But – and this is where the real puzzle sets in – countries that have millions of hungry people are exporting food to countries where people are already well-fed. Why? What kind of a system is this?

Well, it's all to do with 'purchasing power', the citizens of planet Earth might explain. People in rich countries have the money, the purchasing power, to buy food from poor countries, which people in those countries do not have. 'And what are you doing to help them have that purchasing power?' the visitors might ask. 'Well, if these poor countries sell more by trading, they will earn more money and be able to buy more food from abroad,' comes the reply. 'And has this happened in a way that helps the hungry?' 'Well, no, not really, but it might do one day.' In the meantime, the planet Earth has a system which trades its most vulnerable people into hunger.

This account of trade and food security begins in the United States coastal city of Seattle. Trade and agriculture ministers had gone there in November 1999 for a meeting of the World Trade Organization (WTO) that was intended to further the cause of trade liberalization. Yet as the meeting took place there was mounting evidence that such liberalization was failing the most vulnerable members of the global society. To the bewilderment of trade liberalization advocates, the Seattle talks collapsed and did so in quite spectacular fashion. Chapter 1 looks at the details of that collapse. Basically, it came down to a single overriding factor – that there is something wrong with project 'trade liberalization', especially as it affects the food security of the poor. The old argument that free trade will benefit all of us has been proved wrong by the experience of the late twentieth century. While most have gained, the poorest, 800 million hungry people, have lost. Any society, national or international, will ultimately be judged on whether its systems, rules and regulations assist the most needy. By that criterion, the current international trade system is failing. The poor cannot exist on bread that might come one day.

People go hungry because they are too poor to grow enough or to buy enough food. Chapter 2 looks at related factors – poor soils, desertification, the neglect of women farmers, disasters, lack of spending on agriculture, foreign debt, conflict, lack of democracy, climate change, population and land issues, water, loss of crop diversity, inadequate funding for health, and the way that fisheries are under attack. The international community, like many national governments, is failing to accord priority to tackling these problems. In the late 1990s the world as a whole spent more than US$500 billion to combat the supposed 'millennium bug' – ten times more than rich countries give to the poor each year in development assistance. By contrast, the amount needed to halve world hunger by 2015 – a target agreed at the 1996 World Food Summit, as Chapter 2 explains – would be US$60 billion dollars over 15 years, or US$4 billion per year in increased spending, hardly an excessive amount.

The role of trade in the battle against food insecurity is examined in Chapter 3. Trade has raised living standards but it has also caused people to go hungry and even starve. Countries that might have fed themselves have prioritized food exports to better-fed countries. The chapter looks at the Uruguay Round agreement, which brought the WTO into being, and considers the arguments for free trade: that it will lead to higher rates of economic growth, for example, or ensure the best possible use of available resources. It considers why, in today's globalized economy, such arguments are deeply flawed.

Economic globalization and trade liberalization have concentrated power in the larger entities we know as transnational corporations. Small farmers are unable to compete in the global economy and are being driven off their land, leaving the door wide open to the corporations. It is TNCs, not the hungry, who are likely to reap the benefit of modern-day economic growth and liberalization. Free trade has enslaved the hungry rather than freed them. Trade can help to achieve food security, but only if it is democratic and free from corporate control; only if it helps rather than hinders the poor.

Chapter 4 considers the international organizations that have an important influence on trade and food security. Through their introduction of structural adjustment programmes the World Bank and the International Monetary Fund began the contemporary process of trade liberalization in the early 1980s. The liberalization requirements of these SAPs are often harsher than those of the World Trade Organization. But it is now the WTO that sets the rules; this relatively new organization has become the most powerful and dominant player in international trade. The role of United Nations agencies is also considered – especially the UN Conference on Trade and Development (UNCTAD), the world's alternative trade organization. Although

UNCTAD has been sidelined by Western governments, it could have an important role to play.

Evidence of the impact of trade liberalization on food security is revealed in Chapter 5. The evidence – whether from governments or non-governmental bodies – is as startling as it is consistent, yet it is being overlooked by many policy makers. A UN Food and Agriculture Organization study of 16 developing countries found a surge of food imports into these countries in the post-Uruguay Round period, but not an increase in their exports. This is forcing local farmers out of business and the rural areas, leading to a concentration of farm holdings.

NGO studies back up this finding and show what it means to the lives of the poor – how smallholder incomes have fallen and malnutrition among the rural poor has risen. 'Persistent food deficits, decreased incomes, families eating fewer meals each day, poor infrastructure, poor medical services, increased alcoholism, hooliganism and loss of any reasonable protection for farmers, are now characteristic of rural life' – thus runs a fairly typical account of the implications of trade liberalization. These studies show that the 'free trade works for the poor' theory is disproved by what is happening on the ground. Chapter 5 also includes the views of individual farmers, expressed in Seattle at the time of the WTO meeting. Again, there is remarkable consistency – liberalization has damaged their lives. A World Bank study finds that the poorest 40 per cent of people in developing countries have seen their incomes fall since liberalization began. The evidence is powerful and it discredits the claims of Western government ministers that trade liberalization lessens poverty.

The modern world has corporate-managed trade rather than free trade. Chapter 6 looks at corporate influence and power over food and agriculture. Patents, originally designed for mechanical products, are being deployed by TNCs as a powerful weapon for exercising control over agricultural products. The Uruguay Round agreement on Trade-Related Intellectual Property Rights (TRIPs) effectively globalises the patent system. TRIPs has a direct bearing on food security; it means that if a process to produce a plant is patented, the owner of the patent has exclusive rights over the plants obtained using the process. Farmers are then forbidden the use of any seeds coming from such a plant.

The system of intellectual property rights and patents which provides TNCs with the right to patent genetic resources may also encourage monocropping and the spread of genetically uniform trans-genic varieties at the expense of the small farmer. If the international community wants to honour its commitment to reducing the number of hungry people, then it has to give serious consideration to changes in patent rules.

One way in which TNCs hope to benefit from new patents is in the massive expansion of trade in genetically modified foods. These foods have become one of the most controversial issues of our time. Their makers and growers, most of them in the United States, want to trade them. Without trade, their market is too small. In January 2000, as Chapter 7 explains, governments agreed on a protocol that will regulate trade in GM organisms, including foodstuffs. The agreement allows governments to keep out GM foodstuffs as a precaution against environmental, health and other hazards. Agreement on the protocol marks an important step forward in that governments have recognized that free trade should not always be the paramount concern: some human needs are more important.

NGOs are pressing to ensure that food security issues have a central place in the rules that govern international trade. Opposition to the rules and procedures of the WTO is at the heart of NGO objections. Chapter 8 looks at the views of a range of NGOs; there is a wide-spread belief that trade liberalization, and in particular the WTO's Agreement on Agriculture, must be subject to a thorough review and changed if food security is to be advanced. Some NGOs want agriculture to be taken out of the WTO. Dealing with the power of TNCs is again a major issue. These views need to be heard.

Can food security be advanced with less rather than with more trade? Should governments of developing countries put more resources into achieving food security and give less priority to trade? These are questions addressed in the final chapter. In some parts of the develop-ing world, food security is advancing in ways that owe very little to international trade. Chapter 9 looks at how an agriculture that keeps external inputs to a minimum and integrates traditional technologies is raising crop yields. It considers permaculture, a system under which four-fold increases and more in yields have been achieved. It looks at the experience of Cuba, which turned to organic agriculture following the US trade embargo and the collapse of its sugar exports to the former Soviet Union. These examples explode the myth that trade is needed to combat hunger.

Trade liberalization has failed the poor and stands in danger of giving trade as a whole a bad name. The poor are going hungry because of the way the trading system is working. Trade liberalization – 'free' trade, trade without barriers – is harming, not helping them. Instead on relying on free trade dogma, Western governments would do well to look more at what actually works to advance food security.

International trade on the right terms, seen to be fair and democratic, has a role to play in the battle against hunger, in the drive towards food security for the poor. But if trade is to play that role then fundamental changes are needed. Trade, like the WTO, needs to be less dominant; other policies should not be subservient to it. While this represents a big challenge for the international community and national governments, at stake is the commitment to halve the number of people living in hunger by 2015 as a first step towards food security for all. It's a target that must be met.

In 2001, governments are likely to embark on a new round of trade talks. If the poor are to benefit, these talks need to be very different from the agenda that Western countries had in mind in Seattle. Much of the evidence, like many of the ideas and proposals in this book, has been put forward by non-governmental organizations who work alongside the hungry. It is my hope that this account will contribute to shaping a food and trade agenda that does justice to all of humanity.

CHAPTER 1

SEATTLE, 1999

'Only she was from Seattle,
where her daddy raises cattle' –
Guy Mitchell song

Meetings about trade and development issues are usually quite dour affairs and even the more interesting ones are rarely accompanied by massive protests, let alone teargas, bullets and riots. The World Trade Organization's four-day ministerial meeting in Seattle, in late November and early December 1999, was an exception. In its short life, the WTO has aroused huge public concern, not least because of the power that member states have ceded to it and the way that international trade agreements are widening the gap between rich and poor countries. The trade liberalization that the WTO oversees appears to be failing the poor, hindering rather than helping food security, and handing power to transnational corporations.

Preparation

At the WTO's previous ministerial meeting, in Geneva in May 1998, US President Bill Clinton invited the organization's member countries to hold their next ministerial in the US. After the offer was accepted,

US cities competed with each other to host the meeting. The west coast, seaport city of Seattle, in Washington state, won the contest, probably because of its close ties with international trade, and the fact that one in three jobs in the state depends on trade. Microsoft, Boeing and Amazon.com are among the companies based in Seattle.

The Seattle ministerial was preceded by a preparatory period stretching back to early 1999. Through a WTO process called analysis and information exchange (AIE), governments shared in confidence some of their thoughts and views on the key issue of agriculture. These confidential exchanges apart, governments also voiced their opinions publicly. The US and European Union countries, for example, proclaimed that they wanted the Seattle meeting to launch a new round of trade talks to further liberalize trade, although the EU wanted a round with a much wider range of issues than the US had proposed.

Under the AIE process, 45 countries submitted papers. Only eight papers came from developing countries and all showed concern over trade liberalization, highlighting its controversial role in food security. India said in its paper that the 'major thrust' of the WTO's Agreement on Agriculture (see below) 'appears to be based on the hypothesis that liberalization is the panacea for all ills in the agricultural sector'. India urged that developing countries be allowed greater autonomy in establishing and supporting domestic agricultural policy. A purely market-based approach might not be appropriate for developing countries, it said; rather, for some countries, it might be necessary to adopt a

> market-plus approach, in which non-trade concerns such as the maintenance of the livelihoods of the agrarian peasantry and the production of sufficient food to meet domestic needs are taken into consideration.... [W]hile it may not be possible to immediately ensure that developing countries are able to produce at least a minimum percentage of their annual food requirement, this is a goal that has to be pursued.[1]

In a joint paper, Pakistan, Peru and the Dominican Republic argued for consultations to be held on market access, special and differential treatment of developing countries and on the possible negative effects of the Agreement on Agriculture reforms on non-food-importing developing countries. El Salvador, Honduras, Cuba, Nicaragua, Dominican Republic and Pakistan said in another paper that the hoped-for improved market access to developed countries had not materialised. In order to allow 'real and effective market opportunities', future negotiations should take into account the need to 'develop a package of measures aimed at improving the national food security, maintaining the standard of living of the rural population ... and exempt such measures from the reduction commitment.'

Mauritius pressed in its paper for recognition 'to be given to the multifunctional character of agriculture in small island developing states and in small developing countries' – that, in a number of ways, agriculture plays an important role in the economic life of rural areas. It pointed out that while

> it is contended that trade liberalization will impact positively on world markets, this has never been proved.... [T]he WTO is here to enhance welfare, not to promote trade liberalization *per se*. The multi-functional character of agriculture can meet the same objective, i.e. enhanced welfare.

Cuba pointed out that the Agreement 'would be worthless' if, at the end of its implementation, market access had been restricted. It said that it was difficult to contemplate any new commitments unless the effects of commitments so far had been determined.

The AIE process was part of the wider preparatory process for the Seattle meeting, under which more than 80 proposals were submitted to the WTO Committee on Agriculture, 32 of them from developing countries. These proposals were discussed from September 1999 onwards; the aim was to draft a declaration that ministers would simply approve in Seattle. Three months of haggling failed to produce a text; when ministers arrived in the US there was little chance of them being able to reconcile differences. The prospects for launching a new round of trade talks already looked bleak.

Even points of agreement were subject to reservations. Britain's International Development Secretary Clare Short, for example, proposed that the new round be a 'development round' – although with trade liberalization still the central theme. Many developing countries wanted a 'development round' with a rather different emphasis. A number of African civil society organizations viewed the British proposal as a way of winning African countries over to accept the new round of trade negotiations, 'putting a sweetener around the bitter pill of trade liberalization.... [I]t is a ploy to draw the African countries into a new round of trade negotiations to which they are strongly opposed.'[2]

Barrier slashing

The General Agreement on Tariffs and Trade (GATT) Uruguay Round of trade talks, held between 1986 and 1993, led to the setting up of the WTO. The Uruguay Round was the eighth round to be held under the GATT. All the rounds were held with the aim of reducing barriers to trade (see Chapter 3). The Uruguay Round was the first to involve developing countries in significant numbers.

The Uruguay Round agreement not only reduced trade barriers – by an average of 40 per cent – but also laid down rules for what kinds of policies governments can make on matters such as intellectual property and investment, making its impact more complex, more expensive to implement and more difficult to predict. The agreement included agriculture for the first time. But the Agreement on Agriculture is basically a pact between the US and the EU, who rigged the rules to suit themselves. Developing countries had minimal input. The Uruguay Round agreement obliged WTO member countries to review agriculture, services, intellectual property rights (mainly patents) and trade-related investment measures in 2000. These four issues – known as the 'built-in' agenda – would form the core of a new round of trade talks. The question was what precisely the new round would be about, and whether it would include issues such as labour rights, investment, competition policy and environmental standards.

The least-developed and net-food-importing developing countries, hurt by trade liberalization, wanted compensation as laid down in the so-called 'Marrakech decision', which is part of the Uruguay Round agreement, but which had not been implemented by the time of the Seattle meeting. In 1996, when cereal prices rose by over 40 per cent on the previous year, the WTO Committee on Agriculture, on the advice of the IMF, refused to implement the decision. The rise in prices was not considered to be a result of the Uruguay Round agreement. Despite low world food prices in 1998, net-food-importing and least developed countries faced food import bills 20 per cent higher than before the Agreement on Agriculture was implemented. Some countries favoured the automatic and mandatory implementation of the Marrakech decision.

The European Union wanted a new round to cover investment issues but this was seen as a way of reintroducing the discredited Multilateral Agreement on Investment (MAI). This would have removed government regulations on foreign investment, and increased the power of transnational corporations to such an extent that they would have been able to sue governments for introducing environmental or social legislation that might curb their investment. The EU's new trade commissioner, Pascal Lamy, told a meeting of EU trade ministers in October 1999 that something had to be done about investment because 'our enterprises have asked us to act'.[3] It was noted that Lamy did not say that something had to be done because the European public wanted it, but because companies wanted it.

Developing countries overwhelmingly opposed a wider round because of lack of capacity, concern that uncontrolled foreign investment would not benefit them, and the record of the WTO, which they felt was biased towards richer countries and against the poorer. The US appeared to offer African countries an inducement to support its policies. At the end of September 1999, President Clinton announced that the US would cancel the debts owed to it by some of the world's poorest countries, mostly African. He said he was responding to an appeal by the Pope and other religious leaders. The following day a US agriculture official claimed that the US had formed an alliance with sub-Saharan African countries on the Seattle talks. This seemed like an attempt at a deal on debt relief in exchange for African support in the trade talks. It was not to be.

'Stop the Round'

In advance of the Seattle meeting, more than 1,200 NGOs from nearly a hundred countries – from environmentalists to labour unions, Third World development groups to consumer organizations – signed a 'Stop the WTO round' petition. The international trading system, said the petitioners, is 'inequitable, untransparent and in conflict with national and international regimes that promote high environment and development standards'. They proposed a fundamental review of the system, and the development of 'an alternative, humane and sustainable international system of trade and investment relations'. And they urged governments to 'move away from the habit of shaping their international trade policies around the offensive interests of large transnational corporations'.

The week of the ministerial meeting witnessed probably the biggest display of international concern on a social issue since the campaign against apartheid. Over 50,000 people from all over the world came to Seattle to protest about the WTO and the proposal to launch a new round of trade talks. They broadly divided into three groups, with a certain amount of overlap.

The largest number of people were to be found in NGO-organized meetings that were taking place in virtually every hall and church in downtown Seattle. These often packed meetings allowed participants to listen to and share their experience with others, forge alliances and discuss future strategy and tactics. Common to many of these meetings was an unusual degree of enthusiastic optimism among participants, a feeling that they were not just protesting but that their campaigns were making a difference, that their arguments had real force and that they were winning over the official pro-free trade arguments. Their optimism was borne out by events.

Other NGO representatives were inside the conference centre, putting their case to ministers and briefing journalists. They pointed to overwhelming evidence that trade liberalization was instrumental in throwing millions of people in developing countries off their land; that it was hindering, not helping food security; and that it was leading to the concentration of land holdings, making them ripe for corporate takeover. Another dose of the same, another round of barrier slashing, was the very last thing the hungry needed, they believed. And the Uruguay Round was costing poor countries a lot of money, they pointed out, citing a United Nations figure which suggested that developing countries would lose up to US$265 million in export earnings as a result of implementing the agreement.

A third group, also sizeable, had received months of training in non-violent civil disobedience techniques, with the expressed intention of stopping the ministerial meeting from going ahead.

While the 50,000 plus people in Seattle came from many different backgrounds and had differing interests, all were concerned that a new round could lead to a further concentration of power in the hands of transnational corporations and take power away from people. All wanted a moratorium on further liberalization until the WTO system has been fundamentally reformed.

The ministerial meeting attracted so much protest because the WTO 'is seen as standing for the subordination of so many aspects of human existence to trade, as an organization that represents primarily the interests of transnational corporations, and, from the South, as an organization with a very anti-development philosophy,' said Walden Bello, co-director of a Philippines-based NGO, Focus on the Global South.[4]

Three-way split

On the eve of the Seattle ministerial, there was still a serious three-way split between WTO members on agriculture. The US and the 15-strong Cairns group of grain-exporting countries wanted ministers to commit themselves to sweeping away existing barriers to trade in foodstuffs, and to end measures such as export subsidies. The EU and Japan opposed references to the ending of export subsidies and wanted the declaration that emerged from Seattle to recognize the multiple functions that agriculture plays – like providing jobs and stimulating rural economies. The EU also wanted food safety and quality to be mentioned.

Developing countries took the view that they have opened their

markets to foodstuffs but that the EU and US have not done the same
– that the EU has continued to dump its food surpluses on them,
depressing its own agriculture, and that the US has increasingly used
anti-dumping measures against their exports. Developing countries
said that they had been obliged to liberalize far too quickly while
Western countries had taken only minimal steps. 'The nature and pace
of trade liberalization is what is at stake,' said Anthony Hilton, co-
chairman of the economic and trade cooperation negotiating group of
the African, Caribbean and Pacific countries (ACP).[5] They wanted
the right to take measures that would give their agriculture some protection from imports, and to pursue objectives such as food security
and poverty alleviation.

The US administration wanted trade ministers to commit themselves to sweeping away existing barriers to trade in foodstuffs, and
ending measures such as export subsidies. They wanted the Seattle
meeting to be the watershed when nations agreed not just to negotiate
the end of export subsidies on agricultural foodstuffs, but to accept that
there should be no distinction between foodstuffs and industrial
products. The meeting turned out to be a watershed of a different
kind.

This idea of treating food in the same way as any other produce –
the same as waste paper baskets and tin cans, for example – outraged
most of the rest of the world, from the EU to Japan, Africa to Asia.
Food is special, it has a unique role in people's cultures, in people's
security, was the common theme; it cannot be treated as just any other
commodity. Farhad Mahzar, representing a Bangladeshi NGO, spoke
for most of humanity when he told a meeting that 'agriculture is not a
sector of industrial production, it's a way of life'.[6]

But then the United States administration had a problem over
food. Since the WTO was set up in 1995, the US has reduced its
support for farmers and assured them they will be able to sell more
abroad. But such is the nature of some US foodstuffs that few people
abroad want to buy them. US beef, for example, is treated with
hormones, leading to more meat per beast and to a glut of beef which
US farmers are desperate to sell on world markets. European Union
countries, for a start, will not buy it. A great deal of US corn and soya

has been grown from genetically modified seed and again no one is keen to buy it.

The meeting

The WTO is obliged to hold a ministerial meeting every two years. The first, in Singapore (1996), attracted little protest. The second, in Geneva (1998), attracted several thousand protesters who were kept mostly out of the delegates' sight by stringent policing. In Seattle, it was the uninvited guests who turned out to be the most significant – the 50,000-plus people from all over the world who came to protest about WTO's policies.

Before dawn on the opening day of the meeting, thousands of protesters were already on the streets, linking arms and effectively blocking important exits from hotels and entrances to a theatre where the opening ceremonial meeting was due to be held. In Geneva the delegates had hardly seen the protesters; in Seattle the delegates could not get out of their hotels because of them.

Marches began through the streets, bands played and an almost carnival atmosphere prevailed. Music, dancing, chanting, it was all good-humoured and peaceful; looting and rioting did not start until much later in the day and had little to do with the WTO protesters. One woman, wearing a large condom lettered 'Safe Trade', said: 'I think it's important to highlight the fact that the World Trade Organization is taking away every single protective measure we've got. We need to develop a system of safe trade to guarantee the rights of nations to protect their culture as well as their own identity.'[7]

The police, caught unawares, seemed aggrieved that it was the demonstrators who were effectively in charge. 'This is what democracy looks like,' was a frequent chant. Around mid-morning, people who were peacefully linking arms outside a hotel become the first police targets. Teargas was released, pepper was sprayed into people's eyes and rubber bullets were fired. There was no provocation and no attempt to remove people in a peaceful manner. The protests gave the WTO an unusual amount of publicity. Television channels abandoned their normal programmes for several hours to show non-stop coverage of 'the battle of Seattle'. 'Until this week, scarcely anyone in the US had ever heard of the WTO. Now, we know about it and what it stands for,' said a Seattle resident.

The drama was not confined to the streets. In the corridors by the meeting hall some intense lobbying by both voluntary and business NGOs was taking place. 'Of the 1,000 NGOs present in Seattle, at least a third are representing business interests,' said Claire Melamed of Christian Aid. Big business was 'throwing millions of dollars at trying to influence the outcome. This secret world of power makes a mockery of the idea of a fair WTO, accessible to the world's poor.'[8] Big business desperately wanted the Seattle meeting to end with agreement that would give a further push to trade liberalization and ultimately to its profits.

One of the chief business groups active in Seattle was the Transatlantic Business Dialogue, which consists of chief executives of over a hundred large TNCs in the US and the EU. 'This group practically sets the agenda for the WTO,' said Adam Ma'anit of Corporate Europe Observatory. In Seattle, he said, the group tried to bridge 'the divide between the EU and US positions, setting them squarely on a negotiating line that is consistent with the interests of the Microsofts and Nestlés of this world'.[9] Another business grouping lobbying at the meeting was the Union of Industrial and Employers' Confederations of Europe, which consists of 39 central industrial and employers' federations from 31 European countries.

The influence of transnational corporations on the WTO is not sufficiently recognized by governments. Veteran consumer rights activist Ralph Nader, alleged that in effect the corporations have written the WTO rules, and that the world has corporate-managed trade rather than free trade. 'If you have a free trade agreement all you have to do is to have one page saying no more tariffs, no more quotas. But that's not the economic design the global corporations have in mind. They want international patent monopolies, and not just on medicines, on seeds, on flora and fauna; the corporations are writing the rules, and are turning the indentured governments against their own people.'[10]

Inside the meeting hall, the stakes were being raised. WTO

Director-General Mike Moore told ministers that 'this conference is doomed – doomed to succeed'.[11] The reality was very different. Mr Moore would have been wise to omit the end of the sentence.

Proceedings were marked by confusion rather than by an orderly discussion of the issues. Working groups were set up on the opening day – including groups on agriculture, market access and implementation – to help the meeting make progress. Many delegates of developing countries claimed that they were excluded; that their demands were ignored; and that they were kept in the dark about what was happening. One said that his group had met for just 15 minutes; another that a paper produced by the group's chairman, after its discussions, did not reflect the views of developing country delegates. Developing countries alleged that Western countries and WTO chiefs were trying to stitch up the outcome. 'It's as if we do not exist,' said a Namibian delegate, 'there is too much cooking behind the scenes.'[12]

Delegates even tried to get into press conferences to find out what was going on; they were told to wait to see if there was room. Latin American and Caribbean trade ministers spoke of their 'profound surprise and resulting anger' at the organization of the conference.[13] 'African countries were marginalized and excluded,' said John Abu, Ghana's Minister of Trade, on behalf of Organization of African Unity members.[14] Having come to Seattle less than convinced about a new round, ministers of developing countries became even less keen as the week went on. 'Developing countries were marginalized, bullied and ignored,' said Nick Mabey of WWF–UK.[15]

The chairman of the working group on agriculture produced a text which he hoped might serve as a compromise. The text said that negotiations in the new trade round 'shall cover … comprehensive market access leading to the broadest possible liberalization, particularly with regard to products of export interest to developing country members', and aim at 'substantial reductions in all forms of export subsidies … in the direction of progressive elimination of export subsidisation'.[16]

The text also said that 'special and differential treatment for developing countries, as provided for in relevant WTO provisions, shall constitute an integral and effective part of the results of the negotiations ... so as to enable developing countries ... to take account of their development needs, including food security and agricultural and rural development'.[17] While this sounds positive, the 'special and differential treatment' provision in the Uruguay Round agreement has brought few if any benefits to developing countries.

The European Union rejected the text as it was not prepared to support anything that threatened its Common Agricultural Policy. The EU took the view that it did not sufficiently reflect its fundamental positions on maintenance of aid for environmental products, food security, and the economic viability and development of rural regions. It wanted greater emphasis on the need to reduce all forms of farmer supports.

Opposition to the CAP's export subsidies and import barriers united the US administration, developing country governments and development NGOs in both North and South. The US chairman of the Seattle meeting, Charlene Barshefsky, claimed that the CAP was responsible for 85 per cent of the world's agricultural export subsidies – 'the largest distortion of any sort of trade'. The US, however, has replaced export subsidies with direct payments to its farmers, effectively maintaining its overall level of farmer support.

Export subsidies mean that produce, from the EU for example, competes with the produce of farmers in developing countries, while import barriers deprive those farmers of export opportunities. The CAP means that farmers in the EU overproduce; this has led to more food being dumped (sold below the cost of production) in developing countries, undercutting farmers and even forcing them out of business, (see Chapter 4). But the WTO's Agreement on Agriculture did not oblige the EU to change the CAP. The EU was able to claim that it had made the required changes before 1995 (the CAP was last reformed in 1992, and the Agreement's 'reference' period for the reductions was backdated). 'Developed countries have exploited the ambiguous nature of commitments in the Agreement on Agriculture,' said a UK Food Group statement.[18]

In March 1999 heads of EU governments had agreed that grain prices to their farmers should be cut by 15 per cent, in two stages, and that beef prices be cut by 20 per cent, in three stages (over the years

2000–2). To compensate for the reduced prices, however, the EU proposed to increase direct payments to its farmers and effectively provide them with the same income as before. The changes are probably too modest to lower production in the EU and to reduce the impact of the CAP on developing countries.

Apart from crops and livestock, fisheries sectors are usually vital for coastal developing countries but are often undermined by the subsidies paid by Western governments. European Union subsidies for the sector have led to an increase in the EU's sophisticated, high-tech fishing fleets, to the detriment of the fisheries sectors of developing countries. Such subsidies are in contradiction with the European Union Treaty which commits the EU to achieving coherence between fisheries policies and the objectives of EU development policy, namely the eradication of poverty.

In 1998, the EU endorsed a statement of intent at a UN Food and Agriculture Organization meeting to the effect that

> States should reduce and progressively eliminate all factors, including subsidies, and economic incentives which contribute, directly or indirectly, to the build-up of excessive fishing capacity, thereby undermining the sustainability of marine resources, giving due regard to the needs of artisanal fisheries.[19]

The EU has failed to comply.

A number of other issues affecting food security were also a matter of controversy at the Seattle meeting. The EU and the US were split on environmental issues. A US/Canada demand that a Working Party on Biotechnology be established was rejected by EU ministers because they feared it would undermine existing environmentally focused negotiations on regulating GM trade in the BioSafety Protocol under the Convention on Biodiversity. The Working Party would have had a mandate to consider the adequacy and effectiveness of existing rules and the capacity of WTO members to implement these rules. NGOs were opposed to the idea, believing it would have been a step towards freer trade in GM foods.

Forests were an issue of concern especially to environmental NGOs. The US administration pressed for an agreement to scrap tariffs on wood products by the end of 2000 – they labelled this 'accelerated trade liberalization'. The forestry industry had predicted that such a move would increase consumption of wood products by 3 to 4 per cent. As well as more deforestation, this could lead to land that now grows food being planted out with fast-growing trees. The breakdown of the Seattle meeting put a brake on the planned tariff, an outcome welcomed by NGOs.

On TRIPs, a large group of developing countries proposed before the meeting that the declaration to emerge from Seattle should recognize that living organisms and their parts cannot be patented. They claimed that this was consistent with the Convention on Biological Diversity and the International Undertaking on Plant Genetic Resources, and that their proposal would promote the protection of innovations by indigenous and local farming communities; the continuation of traditional farming processes, including the right to use, exchange and save seeds; and, more broadly, the cause of food security. Shortly before the Seattle meeting, however, both the United States and European Union rejected the developing countries' proposals on patenting and references to other international agreements in the draft text.

Neither did the meeting make any progress on labour standards, where strong disagreements emerged between the US and developing countries. Following a 20,000-strong march by US labour unions in Seattle, President Clinton was persuaded to push for labour standards, such as minimum wage levels and a ban on child labour, to be included in WTO rules. The unions are concerned that imported goods made by cheap labour, and even child labour, are losing US jobs.

Developing countries strongly opposed the US stance, seeing it as a form of hidden protectionism and saying that the problem is the poverty that causes parents to send their children out to work. It was also being noted that the US is 'the only country, apart from Somalia, that has not ratified the UN Convention on the Rights of the Child', according to Rita Bhatia of Save the Children.[20] The US stance on workers' rights was a killer blow to the Seattle meeting, as it infuriated ministers of developing countries who were already seething at being left on the sidelines. But the roots went back several weeks. 'Clinton had already sown the seed of the failure in early November when he put on the table the proposal for a WTO working group on labour standards.'[21]

On the second day of the ministerial, chairman Barshefsky had announced her 'right' as chairman to use procedures of her own choosing to get a declaration out of the meeting. Small, so-called 'green room' meetings were set up on key issues but failed to narrow the disagreement. The following day, 'twenty countries received an invitation (at 9.00 pm) for a green room discussion on trade-related intellectual property rights', says Devinder Sharma, an Indian trade policy analyst;

> by two in the morning, some sort of agreement had been reached on the contentious issue. While the United States had agreed to make provision to extend the geographical indicators to cover crops like Basmati rice and Darjeeling tea, in the bargain it had extracted a promise from India and Pakistan to support the formation of the working group on biotechnology. The Africans were obviously angry. None of the African countries was invited to the green room diplomacy. Resenting the undemocratic procedures, the African countries amassed the support of some 100 countries to express their disgust at the way the talks were proceeding and threatened to walk out.[22]

The collapse

In the end, the meeting collapsed in a dramatic manner. Official press conferences had implied that something would be pulled out of the hat, that ministers would not go away empty-handed. But when the final evening came, agreement was nowhere near, and the meeting was 'suspended', in the words of Charlene Barshefsky. In fact, the talks collapsed in chaos, without even a final declaration – not that one could have been agreed. Barshefsky was faced with the prospect that if a draft declaration were presented at a final session, there would be an explosion of protests and a rejection by developing nations. That would have exposed the manipulative methods by which the Seattle conference had been run.

For the US, the EU and the WTO, the collapse was a disaster. But for developing countries the outcome was a relief. 'It is a good outcome,' said an African delegate, while a Middle-Eastern participant was 'very happy'.[23] Three reasons for the failure of the talks were given by Barshefsky – that the issues were very diverse, complex and novel (GM organisms, for example); that the WTO had outgrown processes relevant to an earlier time, making negotiations very difficult to manage; and that divergences remained because countries were not prepared to take difficult political decisions. It was announced that the negotiations would therefore be suspended for a time-out, 'a process that has happened before in the GATT', she claimed.[24]

There were, however, several other reasons. The role of the United States was a major factor. Charlene Barshefsky was both leader of the US and chairman of the meeting. This was a huge procedural mistake. 'The US was a protagonist on a wide range of issues. They did not have that flexibility that we would look towards from a chairman to bring about some agreement,' said Kibsul Cisutikul, Thailand's Director of Economic Affairs.[25]

The talks collapsed partly because the US and the EU failed to agree on agriculture. There were also other unresolved issues between them – such as industrial tariff negotiations, rules on environment and biotechnology, implementation of existing agreements, and the question of whether investment and competition should be included in a new round of negotiations. But there were other, more significant reasons for the collapse.

Developing countries felt uneasy about the pace of trade liberalization; they were infuriated by the US stance on labour rights; and they felt alienated from the discussions, not just in Seattle but also in the preparatory period. 'The untransparent nature of the WTO system and its blatant manipulation by the major powers' are cited by Martin Khor of the Malaysia-based Third World Network as the basic causes of the collapse:

the seeds of discord were sown in Geneva in the weeks before Seattle. Developing countries voiced disappointment that five years after the WTO's creation they had not seen promised benefits. They put forward dozens of proposals, including changing some of the rules. Most of their demands were dismissed. The major economies pushed instead their own proposals to further empower the WTO by intro-ducing new areas such as investment, competition, government pro-curement, and labour and environmental standards.[26]

This brought no credit to either the US or the WTO and may have even sowed the seeds of the WTO's ultimate demise.

Charlene Barshefsky's analysis that the meeting was a failure of governments, rather than a victory for protesters, did not stand up. 'The impact of grassroots protests against globalization, already evident in the campaigns on the Multilateral Agreement on Investment and against genetic engineering, had its coming-of-age in the street battles of Seattle,' believes Khor.[27] The impact was considerable and possibly all-important. Earlier in the week, it looked as though the developing countries might possibly give in to all-embracing US pressure ('You won't be our friend if you don't see it our way'). Ministers from developing countries were encouraged by the anti-WTO protests and became determined to stand up for what they believed in.

The protesters did make a difference. In the words of one of their chants, 'The people came and stole the show'. The opposition of civil society 'encouraged different countries to register their dissatisfaction with and oppose various elements of proposed negotiations ... it became easier for governments to resist the usual pressures to conform,' said Friends of the Earth.[28] African countries, 'despite their pathetic economies had mustered enough courage and support to thwart the biggest trade talks of the century.'[29]

The significance of the outcome of the Seattle meeting was that it represented 'a spectacular derailment of the free trade juggernaut'.[30] 'The Seattle fiasco has driven the first nail in the coffin of the WTO,' believes Devinder Sharma.[31] Others were striking a more cautious note.

It is too early to say for certain whether Seattle is a temporary setback for the WTO, a permanent weakening of its influence, or an opening to advance progressive reforms in global governance. Certainly, Seattle was a serious challenge to the WTO's legitimacy and the next years will be a critical period for the organization.[32]

The collapse in Seattle slowed down the trade liberalization project. It 'has demonstrated that globalization is not an inevitable phenomenon ... but a political project which can be responded to politically'.[33] The collapse provides a breathing space for a hard look at just exactly what trade liberalization has meant for the lives of the poor and what its implications are for food security.

Postscript

Within days of Seattle, the European Commission, urged on by transnational corporations, was speaking of its wish to resume negotiations. These are likely to be delayed at least until the WTO's Fourth Ministerial Conference in 2001. At a meeting in February 2000, the General Council of the WTO decided that discussions on agriculture and services – part of the Uruguay Round's 'built-in agenda' – should proceed. These will lack clear guidelines, but some initiatives may move forward – market access for the least developed countries, for example. The EU, Brazil and some African countries are likely to push for a special conference in 2000 focused on reforming the workings of the WTO in order to increase efficiency, transparency and accountability.

In February 2000 the WTO was reported to be trying to put together a package for the 48 least developed countries (LDCs) that would give their products unrestricted access to the markets of Western countries. This move 'is an attempt to win the backing of the LDCs for a new round of global trade negotiations'.[34] And NGOs continued to question the dominance of trade, especially over food and agricultural issues, and the dominance of the WTO over trade.

CHAPTER 2

FOOD SECURITY

'Being rich means having enough food for the whole year' –
Nepalese peasant
quoted in Good Aid *(D. Millwood and H. Gezelius)*

Food is more than a commodity that is bought and sold. It is more than the nutrients that we consume. Food meets many kinds of human needs – cultural, psychological and social among them. It is *the* social good. 'Food is a feeling; it's in the imagination; it binds people. Food is the point of reference which everyone can recognize and share.'[1] Lack of food is the ultimate exclusion. When people don't have food they are excluded from what the rest of society is doing regularly – eating.

Food is the good that keeps us alive, the overriding human need, the very means of life, recognized in the charter of the United Nations as a human right. While people do not live by bread, rice, sorghum or cassava alone, food makes it possible for people to start and continue life. Lack of food brings about pain, suffering, illness and death; it causes most of the world's killer diseases; it means that parents watch in powerless anguish as their children die. *Food is special; it is totally different from any other commodity.*

Agriculture is likewise more than just another economic activity. In developing countries it employs the great majority of people.

Agriculture is a way of life that services a deep human need and performs a variety of different functions – not just producing crops and animals but also providing jobs and stimulating rural economics. It also contributes to the environment, with farmers having a key role to play as stewards of land and the wider environment. Agriculture has an overriding claim to be dealt with differently from industrial production and services. This is recognized by almost all the world's governments.

Famine is something that makes news. Hunger, lack of food security, is something that is chronic, ongoing, a daily fact of life for millions which rarely makes news because it is not new. At a personal level, lack of food security can mean that people cannot eat every day, let alone a good meal every day. At the start of the third millennium, many millions of people lack enough nutritious food to live healthy lives. Some 790 million do not have food security, according to the FAO. South Asia contains 283.9 million hungry people; East and Southeast Asia, 241.6 million; sub-Saharan Africa, 179.6 million; Latin America, 53.4 million; the Near East and North Africa, 32.9 million. Over 20,000 people a day are dying from the effects of hunger. Even though in some areas output per hectare is low, lack of food overall is not caused by the lack of production but by low incomes and unequal access to resources such as land, water, credit and markets.

When government leaders met at the World Food Summit (WFS) in November 1996, they made a commitment to halve the number of hungry people in the world by 2015, as a first step towards the goal of food for all. They ended the Summit by approving the Rome Declaration on World Food Security and Plan of Action to combat hunger. Food security is defined in the Declaration as: 'food that is available at all times, to which all persons have means of access, that is nutritionally adequate in terms of quantity, quality and variety, and is acceptable within the given culture'. The cost would amount to US$60 billion over 15 years, or US$4 billion per year in increased spending.

'We, the Heads of State and Government, or our representatives, reaffirm the right of everyone to have access to safe and nutritious food, consistent with the right to adequate food and the fundamental right of everyone to be free from hunger,' says the Declaration:

we pledge our political will and our common and national commitment to achieving food security for all and to an ongoing effort to
eradicate hunger in all countries, with an immediate view to reducing
the number of undernourished people to half their present level no
later than 2015. We consider it intolerable that more than 800 million
people throughout the world, and particularly in developing
countries, do not have enough food to meet their basic nutritional
needs. This situation is unacceptable.... The problems of hunger and
food insecurity have global dimensions and are likely to persist, and
even increase dramatically in some regions, unless urgent, determined
and concerted action is taken, given the anticipated increase in the
world's population and the stress on natural resources.

These commitments may be less than binding, but they are nonetheless important markers. Governments are expected to keep them;
the world is watching to see that they do. But for the commitments to
become reality, more priority and resources will be needed. And yet
the hunger problem 'may get worse before it gets better', warns
Indian scientist, M. S. Swaminathan, since 'neither global nor macro-
economic policies are in favour'.[2] Many governments do not yet have
the policies to match their commitments, while the international
economic environment is hardly favourable.

Progress in the first two years after the World Food Summit was
mixed. In November 1998, an FAO paper warned that

progress is not being made at anywhere near the rates required for
meeting the Summit target. Unless major efforts are made to improve
food supplies, as well as to overcome inequalities, some countries may
still have an incidence of undernutrition ranging from 15 to 30 per
cent of their populations.

The world has the capacity to produce the additional food needed to
eliminate undernutrition, the paper went on. 'The persistence of
hunger is due to development failures.'[3]

In October 1999, the FAO put a more encouraging slant on the
figures.

Since 1990/92, the number of people going hungry in developing

countries has declined by 40 million. Malnourishment fell in 37
countries between 1990/92 and 1995/97. But the number of hungry
people in developing countries remains unacceptably high, at 790
million.[4]

The findings of the report suggest nonetheless that at the current rate
of progress – 8 million fewer undernourished people each year – the
World Food Summit's goal of halving the number of hungry people
in the world by 2015 will not be reached. Some regions, however,
have made impressive progress over the past two decades, demonstrat-
ing that hunger is not an intractable problem.

But another report two years after the Summit – the findings of a
study on global warming – makes for disturbing reading. It suggests
that climate change will cause severe drought conditions in parts of
Africa by 2050. An additional 30 million Africans could be affected by
famine 'because of the reduced inability to grow crops in large parts of
Africa'.[5] If this calculation is correct, the world will have to run even
faster to ensure that Africa has a buffer against this threat.

The two years after the Summit were also marked by financial
turmoil in Asia, which threatened to reverse some of the economic
gains made by Asian countries in the fight against hunger. Millions of
people lost their jobs and livelihoods in the economic downturn; they
returned to their rural areas which no longer received remittances from
their comparatively well-off relatives in the city. They also had to cope
with soaring prices of basic foodstuffs and agricultural inputs, again
caused by the crisis. In Indonesia, the percentage of people living
below the poverty line declined from 60 per cent in 1970 to 11 per
cent in 1996. But between 1996 and the end of 1998 10 million
people lost their jobs in the financial crisis and poverty increased six-
fold. Inevitably, those worst affected were already vulnerable to hunger.

Food insecurity

Food insecurity for many millions of people arises for a number of
reasons, but the overrriding reason is poverty. 'Poverty is an insult,'
said Mahatma Gandhi, 'poverty stinks. It demeans, dehumanises,

destroys the body and the mind ... if not the soul. It is the deadliest form of violence.' People go hungry because they are too poor to grow enough or to buy enough food; they do not have the money to exercise effective demand in a free market. Millions of the rural poor are either landless or have only very small plots of land on which they can grow little. To survive they need to buy food. But their poverty means they do not have the purchasing power to buy the food that is available. People can go hungry in villages even when their local markets are brimming over with food. In most rural areas, there are few jobs outside agriculture and the growth rate in rural non-farm employment is slow. This means that few have the chance to earn a wage and an income to enable them to buy the food they need.

In addition to the inability of the poor to buy food, the poverty that causes hunger also arises from the inability of farmers 'to get hold of technologies or approaches that could improve farming, without recourse to large amounts of money'.[6] Farmers often cannot grow enough food to last their families for a whole year. Several hungry months of the year are often the result. About 1,400 million in developing countries make a living from small-scale farming. These farmers are overwhelmingly resource-poor. Their land is often in marginal areas, where precipitation is inadequate and fragile soils are vulnerable to erosion, and where desertification may pose a serious threat. Their small-holdings, low yields, lack of productive services and weak, inefficient markets for inputs and produce bind these farmers in a low-production, low-savings trap.

Hopes that the so-called 'green revolution' of the 1960s – the application of fertiliser and water to higher-yielding crop varieties – would lead to sustainably high yields have now been dashed. In many green revolution states of India, for example, yields appear to have peaked, and are going down in some areas, due to soil deterioration. Ironically, however, the world now produces more food per inhabitant than ever before. Enough is available to provide 4.3 pounds to every person every day: 2.5 pounds of grain, beans and nuts, about a pound of meat, milk and eggs, and another of fruits and vegetables. This is enough to give everyone an adequate diet.

'Food sovereignty' is another concept which has entered the food

debate. This goes a step further than food security and might broadly
be defined as countries and communities having the democratic right
and power to determine the production, distribution and consumption of food according to their preferences and cultural traditions. The
food sovereignty concept places less emphasis on trade.

Poor soils

If food insecurity, or lack of food sovereignty, is caused by poverty,
this condition in turn is exacerbated by other factors. Poor, infertile
soils often explain why small farmer production is limited. Around 14
per cent of land in developing countries is used to grow crops or horticultural produce for export, and the amount of land under export
crops is expanding. This is invariably the best land. Small-scale farmers
are often pushed onto more fragile land with poor soils.

Often these soils are not only poor, but also eroding. Since the
1950s over a fifth of agricultural land worldwide has been degraded.
'Soil erosion is by far the most widespread cause of degradation....
There is widespread evidence of erosion resulting in losses greatly in
excess of 50 tons of soil per hectare per year, losses that may be five or
more times the natural rate of soil formation.'[7]

Causes of soil infertility include shortage of manure, tilling practices, continuous cropping of the same land, limited crop rotation,
overgrazing and the indiscriminate cutting of trees. African soils are of
particular concern.

> The depletion of nutrients from soils has caused crop production to
> stagnate or decline in many African countries. Unless African govern-
> ments, supported by the international community, take the lead in
> confronting the problems of nutrient depletion, deteriorating agricul-
> tural productivity will seriously undermine the foundations of sustain-
> able economic growth in Africa.[8]

Desertification

Linked to poor soils is the problem of desertification or land degradation. This is estimated to be driving around three million people a

year from their rural homes and into towns and cities; their land can no longer support them. Living in dryland areas, often on the fringes of deserts, they are overwhelmingly among the world's poorest people. Almost one in six of the world's population are affected, some 900 million people.

Desertification results from a number of factors, including climatic variations and human activities such as overgrazing and excessive firewood cutting. When their land becomes barren and unable to produce food, the poor have no option but to move on. Home to some of the world's poorest people, the Sahel region of Africa is particularly affected. Lying south of the Sahara desert, the region stretches from Mauritania on the Atlantic to Ethiopia on the Red Sea. Many millions of people from the Sahel have become 'land refugees' in the last 20 years, and been forced to move south towards the West African coastline. People forced off their land may go to other rural areas, putting those areas in turn at risk of degradation.

Although poor people in marginal environments 'have a remarkable capacity to cope with food shortages', coping systems are beginning to break down, with successive droughts pushing communities into a downhill spiral.[9] In Burkina Faso, for example, people have migrated from the country's degraded central plateau to the humid south, causing serious tensions and putting additional strain on already over-stretched services and resources. Africa north of the Sahara is also affected, with desertification a severe problem for countries such as Algeria and Morocco. Many farmers in India have been forced by inhospitable land to move from western Rajasthan and eastern parts of the country to neighbouring Haryana and Madhya Pradesh. Some of them have made their way to Madras, overburdening basic services such as water supplies. Some of the huge and growing cities in Latin America are due to the influx of farmers whose land could no longer yield them a living.

In some areas the problems are being tackled successfully. Clusters of trees, for example – so called 'shelterbelts' – are appearing in parts of the Sahel to shield food-growing land from the desert. But some farmers are reluctant to invest in such measures because they do not have secure tenure to the land they farm.

Desertification has been called 'a global problem with local solutions'. Local people need support from governments and the international community – especially funds, technology, information, and assistance for overcoming poverty. As the Group of 77 developing countries told the United Nations General Assembly in October 1998, 'the eradication of poverty remains the key to combating desertification'.

Neglect of women farmers

Women farmers produce a large proportion of the world's food – 80 to 90 per cent in sub-Saharan Africa, 50 to 90 per cent in Asia, 30 per cent in Central and Eastern Europe, according to FAO estimates. 'There will be no food security without rural women', says FAO Director-General Jacques Diouf.[10]

Yet women farmers are often neglected by (usually male) policy makers. The particular circumstances and problems they face are overlooked. They have difficulty obtaining credit facilities in many countries, partly because they are not legally allowed to own land – land rights in most developing countries do not extend to rights for women. Their output of subsistence foods, if it does not enter the market, may not count in national income statistics. Their contribution is therefore not properly valued and understood. In no country is the potential of women farmers being realized.

The 1996 World Food Summit declaration recognized that the limited access of rural women to productive resources and their restricted role in policy and economic decision making contribute to poverty and are obstacles to food security; that policies and programmes in many countries pay little heed to equality between men and women; and that the absence of gender-disaggregated information and data prevents informed social and economic decision making.

Women not only grow food, but are also responsible in many countries for post-harvest processing and marketing. They are always responsible for food safety and for trying to meet the nutritional needs of their families. Although they produce most of the food in developing countries, food insecurity is often more acute for females.

In the family situation in many countries, males receive a bigger share of the food than females. Women account for 60 per cent of the Third World poor; they account for two-thirds of the world's illiterates – fewer girls than boys go to school. In turn, this can mean that women are less aware of their rights.

Disasters

Agriculture is being interrupted more frequently by 'natural' disasters. According to the *World Disasters Report*, they were responsible for 'creating 58 per cent of the world's refugees' in 1999, more than ever before.[11] Most disasters are of human rather than natural origin. Deforestation strips hillsides bare and makes mudslides more likely – as thousands of people in Venezuela, Honduras, Guatemala, Nicaragua and other countries found to their cost in the late 1990s.

Underfunded agriculture

Many developing countries have neglected their agricultural sectors, devoting only a small proportion of available resources to them. Agriculture is seen as a less glamorous activity than industry. International research institutes that are trying, for example, to develop drought-proof crops have had their funding squeezed. The Ibadan-based International Institute of Tropical Agriculture has developed drought-tolerant maize varieties but has had to lay off staff because of funding problems. Yet the agricultural sector cries out for more spending and greater priority if disasters are to be avoided.

Foreign debt

By the mid-1990s foreign debt had emerged as one of the biggest single factors keeping people in poverty and hunger. High levels of foreign indebtedness mean that countries have to switch money away from agriculture and other essentials in order to make debt repayments. African countries are severely affected by this.

Third World debt grew from US$9 billion in 1955 to US$572 billion in 1980 and to over US$2,200 billion in 1998. Servicing those debts – repaying interest and capital – costs developing countries over US$200 billion a year – four times as much as they receive in development aid. The money is owed to Western countries, international aid agencies, the IMF and banks. Over 50 countries, mostly African, are carrying severe debt burdens and sub-Saharan Africa's foreign debt is over three times greater than its annual exports.

The human cost of this debt burden is enormous. The 1997 *Human Development Report* estimated that if severely indebted countries were relieved of their annual debt repayments they could use funds for investments 'that in Africa alone would save the lives of about 21 million children by 2000 (seven million lives a year) and provide 90 million girls and women with access to basic education'.[12] With more of their own funds to invest, the indebted countries would be less dependent on investments from transnational corporations.

In 1996 the IMF and the World Bank launched a modest scheme, the Heavily Indebted Poor Countries Debt Initiative. Very few countries qualified and only after meeting strict economic conditions. But by early 2000 progress was being made on debt relief, chiefly because of a well-organized civil society campaign. The London-based Jubilee 2000 Coalition, a global network of NGOs, campaigned vigorously in the late 1990s for the debts of poor countries to be wiped out in the year 2000 as a fitting way to mark the new millennium.

When leaders of seven large industrial nations met in Cologne in June 1999, they agreed to cancel US$100 billion (out of US$370 billion owed by the 52 poorest countries) of Third World debt. In September, President Clinton announced that the US would cancel all the interest and capital owed on development assistance and commercial debt. In all, some US$6 billion of debt would be cancelled. In December 1999, Britain and Italy made similar announcements, with France following suit in January 2000.

The offers are tied to the IMF/World Bank HIPC initiative. They only become operative when the Fund and the Bank finalize debt relief packages for the indebted countries. The money cancelled must be used for poverty alleviation, thus overcoming the criticism that it might be used by governments for other purposes, such as purchasing armaments. About 40 countries seem likely to receive a degree of debt cancellation by the end of the year 2000, but for some of them the amount of relief will be quite small. Many will still be paying more on debt repayments than they do on health-care services and education.

Conflict

Often caused by poverty, conflict is a major reason why people go hungry. War-torn countries such as Liberia, Somalia, Sierra Leone, Rwanda and Burundi are among the world's hungriest; all witnessed gruesome civil wars in the late twentieth century, causing hundreds of thousands of deaths and severe food shortages. 'Acute [food] shortages, or famines, are almost always conflict-related,' says a *World Disasters Report*.[13]

Wars demand money which could have been used for boosting food output. They disrupt food supply distribution and cause havoc for agriculture. Land is damaged, farmers may be unable to buy seed for planting, harvests plummet. Instead of crops, it is land mines which are often 'planted' in war situations. 'In some countries as much as 35 per cent of arable land cannot be used because of mines,' says *World Disasters*. Food shortages occur as people flee from their land or are afraid to farm it.

Democracy

Democracy is often a casualty of conflict. Severe food shortages, famine and internal unrest are more likely in countries where political systems do not function properly. Democracy encourages a government to act on matters of public concern; if it doesn't, it may lose power to an opposition party. Democracy also encourages a free press, which can report on food shortages and expose inadequate food security policies.

Climate change

Global warming, caused largely by carbon emissions (10 per cent of
which are emitted by five giant oil companies), is set to have a huge
impact on agriculture and food security. Variability in agricultural production is already a key factor in food insecurity. Some areas of the
world are particularly prone to such variability – the Sahel region of
Africa, northeast Brazil, Central Asia and Mexico, for instance.
Climate change is likely to exacerbate this. Yields of corn, soya beans
and wheat, both rainfed and irrigated, could be lower and more
variable. The ranges and populations of agricultural pests may change.
For livestock, higher temperature may increase diseases and heat stress.

Harsher and more extreme weather is likely to result from global
warming. 'It is likely that higher temperatures will produce more
intense atmospheric circulation and a faster water cycle, leading to
heavier and more erratic rains, stronger winds and more frequent
floods,' believes the FAO.[14] Erratic rains could also lead to more
droughts. Demand for water for irrigation is likely to rise in the warmer
climates, putting scarce water supplies under pressure. Fluctuations in
the weather could put additional stress on fragile farming systems,
making land degradation more likely.

Low-lying areas of coastal countries will be especially affected by
rising sea levels. Salty sea water will seep into ground water, thus
providing a difficult environment for crop growth. A sizeable part of
world food production comes from these areas. In densely populated,
low-lying areas of countries such as Bangladesh, China, Egypt,
Indonesia and Malaysia there could be huge damage to crops. Most
existing crop varieties cannot cope with saline conditions and agriculture could become difficult to sustain. Sea-level rises could affect fish
and prawn production worldwide. Some island countries, in the
Pacific for example, could be submerged if levels rise by more than a
metre, while others will be affected by the flooding of fields. Rice, the
chief staple food for many millions of people, is particularly vulnerable. According to a study by the UN Environment Programme, rice
production in Malaysia, for example, could fall by more than 20 per
cent over the next 30 years.

For subsistence farmers, and especially for people who now face a shortage of food, lower yields caused by climate change could result in economic losses, malnutrition and famine. The World Bank and other multilateral agencies have urged that climatic forecasts be made available to small-scale farmers 'to increase food security'. But there are huge practical difficulties – resource-poor farmers are unlikely, for a start, to pursue a strategy that assumes a forecast will be correct.[15] And knowing that flooding is going to occur, for example, will be scant comfort to farmers who do not have the resources to take evasive action or to move elsewhere.

Population and land

While generally the fears expressed by the Reverend Thomas Malthus in the eighteenth century have proved unfounded, population growth is putting pressure on key resources such as land in some countries. Malthus believed that population would increase at a much faster rate than food output. At the global level his theory has been proved wrong. There is no relationship between the prevalence of hunger in a country and its population. For every densely populated and hungry nation like Bangladesh or Haiti, there is a sparsely populated and hungry nation like Brazil and Indonesia. The world today produces more food per inhabitant than ever before.

While population growth was steep in the latter half of the twentieth century – rising from 3 billion in 1960 to 6 billion in 1999 – the world's production of food more than doubled in these 40 years, keeping well ahead of population growth. In many sub-Saharan African countries, however, although population growth rates are falling, they are still higher than the rate of growth of food supply. It is estimated that between 2000 and 2050 global population will increase from 6 billion to 8.5–9 billion people. Most of the additional population will be in developing countries. This will inevitably put land under pressure. In some countries, the key question is whether there will be enough land to grow the food that people need.

But population growth is not the only pressure on land. Expansionist agribusinesses, including transnational corporations, are pushing small farmers off their land and into the towns. Forced to compete with high-yielding varieties produced on large monocropped farms, for example, many subsistence farmers are losing their livelihoods and being plunged into hunger and poverty.

In some areas, shortage of labour to work the land is threatening to cause food shortages. In a number of sub-Saharan African countries, the farming population is declining because of HIV/Aids. In Uganda, for example, the disease has led to a shortage of young farmers in some parts of the country and this could seriously hamper the production of food.

Water

Water scarcity may ultimately lead to food scarcity. Resource-poor farmers often lack access to irrigation facilities or other water sources; their crops are dependent on rainfall. This means there may be no possibility of growing more than one crop a year. Farmers without adequate water sources may be reluctant to plant higher-yielding crops which need water, such as maize, for fear of drought. They are left with less nutritious crops such as cassava, millet and sorghum, which can survive in drought conditions.

At the start of the third millennium, 31 countries with a collective population of half a billion people are experiencing chronic water shortages. Within 25 years the figure is expected to explode to 3 billion in close to 50 countries. More irrigation is however unlikely be the answer. Most existing irrigation is costly and inefficient, and puts groundwater under considerable pressure. Aquifers are already drying up in some parts of the Middle East. Frequent breakdowns and poor maintenance of the water pumps can also hamper food production. Pumps designed with little thought for or consultation with users are a further contributory factor.

Especially worrying is the overpumping of underground waters in some countries. According to the International Water Management Institute, 'water in India is being pumped at twice the rate it is being replenished by rainfall'.[16] The consequence, it speculates, could be a reduction of a quarter in India's harvest, at a time when the country's population is increasing by 100 million people every decade. Preferable to and more affordable than irrigation facilities are improved facilities for water harvesting, collection and storage. More farmers are likely to turn to such methods as water becomes ever scarcer.

Crop diversity

A diverse variety of plants, both wild and cultivated, is essential if crops are to be developed which yield more, resist pests and disease, and tolerate difficult environments. The chief cause of the decline is the replacement of local crop varieties, which is a direct result of green revolution technology. Humankind has become dangerously dependent on a small number of crops. 'The genetic diversity of our critical plant species is disappearing at a terrible pace,' says a report by the Crucible Group, made up of experts from South and North.[17] The FAO estimates that over the last 100 years around three-quarters of the world's known plant species have been lost.

According to the Global Biodiversity Assessment of the United Nations Environment Programme (UNEP), 5 to 20 per cent of plant species are threatened with extinction in the foreseeable future unless present trends are reversed. The survey says not only that many plants are at risk, but also that habitats are being lost at 'much higher than previous rates'. The assessment warns that the loss of diversity 'threatens humanity's food supplies'.[18] The loss also threatens health. Many of the traditional rices in India that were lost in the green revolution's push for higher-yielding rices contained considerable amounts of Vitamin A in their grain, a vital vitamin for health (see Chapter 7).

The threat to species has never been greater, stresses Elizabeth Dowdeswell, UNEP's former Executive Director, and 'there are indications that humanity is now on the verge of a new wave of massive extinctions'.[19] Up to 70 per cent of tropical plants could become extinct in the next 20 to 30 years. Properly managed and used sustainably, these resources need not be depleted.

Health cuts

Many health-care services, especially in rural areas, have been starved of funds in recent years, largely because of government spending cutbacks to meet the demands of structural adjustment programmes. The World Bank has identified 44 countries that do not have the resources to provide basic health-care services; these include practically every country in sub-Saharan Africa. This inevitably affects health. Disease weakens people and often makes it difficult for them to farm. HIV/Aids is possibly the most serious example of this. Victims are often too weak for farming tasks – a huge problem in Southern Africa where it chiefly affects a generation of young people, both farmers and urban dwellers, lowering food output, distorting distribution networks and consumption patterns, and generally disrupting internal food markets.

Local fisheries scooped

Fish contributes a significant amount of animal protein to the diets of people worldwide; it is highly nutritious and serves as a valuable supplement in diets lacking essential vitamins and minerals. Between 15 and 20 per cent of all animal proteins come from fish. As well as being a vital food, it is also a source of work and money for millions of people around the globe. At least 200 million fishworkers depend both directly and indirectly on fishing for their livelihoods, 95 per cent of them in developing countries. The majority of these men, women and children earn their living from fishery-related activities in small-scale, traditional or artisanal fishing communities.

But fisheries in many developing countries are under threat, especially from foreign trawlers. Trawlers from the European Union, for example, have been enabled by generous subsidies to use more sophisticated fishing techniques and increase their capacity in West African waters. While the trawlers have to keep at least 10 kilometres from the coast, they can scoop up fish which swim in and out of the coastal zone to the detriment of local fishermen. The result is that catches are declining for local people. This diversion of fish from local communities and developing regions can deprive hungry people of a traditionally cheap but highly nutritious food.

Conclusion

All the above factors contribute to food insecurity in developing countries. But the international community, like many national governments, is not according enough priority to tackling these problems. Funding is inadequate and, in the case of climate change, Western governments provide insufficient encouragement for people to change lifestyles and use substantially less energy.

Instead of giving higher priority to solving these complex problems of food insecurity, many Western countries and international institutions, such as the WTO, too often give the impression that they have only one shot in the locker – trade liberalization. This, they seem to believe, is the key to ending hunger. As the twenty-first century dawned, however, there was growing recognition among governments of developing countries and non-governmental organizations, if not among Western governments, that trade liberalization was not the solution but the problem.

CHAPTER 3

TRADE LIBERALIZATION

'Globalization of food markets is an instant strategy
for creating hunger' –
Vandana Shiva

International trade in foodstuffs has been going on for many hundreds of years. Historically the trade has taken place because one country wanted to buy a food that it could not produce itself – a temperate zone country cannot produce bananas, for example. It has also taken place because one country could produce food more cheaply than another. In the nineteenth century, the trade increased when some of the best land in colonized Africa, Asia and Latin America was used to grow food for export to the metropolitan economies.

The trade grew slowly in the 30 years following the Second World War but increased rapidly in the last quarter of the twentieth century. As a result of successive rounds of trade liberalization and the trend towards globalization – the integration of the world economy – international trade expanded far more quickly than the rise in food output. Again, in the late twentieth century expanded trade helped countries such as China, South Korea and others in East Asia to reduce malnutrition and poverty.

And yet trade is a highly controversial weapon in the battle against food insecurity; it has both raised living standards and caused people to go hungry and even starve. During Ireland's famine of 1846–7, for example, which killed almost a million people, 'large landowners routinely exported food to Britain as poor peasants dropped all around them'.[1] Substitute Ireland for developing countries, large landowners for transnational corporations, and Britain for the Western world, and little has changed. Food is still being exported from countries where there is gross hunger and people are dropping as a result.

Yet the UN Food and Agriculture Organization, which has a mandate to 'raise levels of nutrition and standards of living' has never been slow to put the case for trade: 'Without trade, countries would have to rely exclusively on their own production; overall incomes would be far lower, the choice of goods would be far less and hunger would increase.' But the FAO adds that the relation of trade to food security raises a number of complex issues and that the expansion in the volume of trade 'has been accompanied by declining terms of trade for the products of developing countries, which have eroded possible gains considerably'.[2] According to the 1996 World Food Summit declaration, 'Trade is a key element in achieving food security; we agree to pursue food trade and overall trade policies that will encourage our producers and consumers to utilise available resources in an economically sound and sustainable manner.'

A country that increases earnings from trade has more resources, in theory, to fight poverty. In practice, however, such resources may be used elsewhere. But a country that puts more resources into trade may have fewer resources for producing its own food. It also becomes more vulnerable to factors outside its control; changes in the agricultural and trading practices of developed countries can have a big impact on developing countries. And it is abundantly clear that more food traded does not mean more food grown or more food for the hungry.

Trade carried out on fair terms can help the poor to increase their incomes. But trade liberalization of the kind that was common in the last two decades of the 1900s has been seen to hit the poor and has damaged trade's contribution to food security. The key question is put in an FAO report: 'While more liberal trade policies over time contribute to economic growth, the main issue for food security is whether this economic growth reaches the poor' (see below).[3]

Trade liberalization – the reduction of barriers to trade – has been under way for manufactured goods since the late 1940s. In 1947 the General Agreement on Tariffs and Trade was signed by 23 countries. The agreement was basically a code of rules for international trade; its aim was 'to provide a secure and predictable international trading environment'. GATT's member countries set about the task of reducing barriers to trade and between 1947 and 1979 held seven 'rounds' to liberalize trade in manufactured goods.

In 1986 a new round of talks was launched, the Uruguay Round, with GATT members deciding to include agriculture (and also services) for the first time. Trade liberalization of agricultural produce was by then already under way in developing countries. It had begun in earnest in the early 1980s with the introduction of structural adjustment programmes by the IMF and the World Bank. The Fund and the Bank insisted that developing countries 'structurally adjust' their economies if they wanted development aid or assistance with overcoming balance of payments problems. SAPs were effectively a new form of economic colonialism. Trade liberalization is central to these programmes and so became a central feature of the economic policies of most developing countries.

The Agreement on Agriculture

The Uruguay Round of negotiations ended in 1993 with a number of agreements – notably the Agreement on Agriculture. This is basically a pact between the US and the EU; developing countries had minimal input. When the negotiations were floundering in 1992, US and EU negotiators met in Washington and came up with the Blair House agreement, on which the Agreement on Agriculture is based. The GATT Uruguay Round also ushered in the WTO, which is a kind of expanded GATT with a great deal more power.

The Agreement on Agriculture covers three main areas – market access, export subsidies and domestic support for agriculture. Under the Agreement, WTO's member countries are obliged to provide minimum access for agricultural produce they do not export in significant quantities. Developed countries have to allow minimum access of 3 per cent of domestic consumption, rising to 5 per cent by 2000. For developing countries the figures are 1 per cent and 4 per cent.

Countries were obliged under the Agreement to reduce tariffs on imported food by 36 per cent over 6 years (beginning in 1995) and also to convert non-tariff barriers, like quota restrictions, into tariffs – so-called 'tariffication'. For developing countries the required reduction was 24 per cent, which could be spread over ten years. Countries also had to cut export subsidies to their farmers by 36 per cent over six years. Again for developing countries the required reduction was 24 per cent, spread over ten years. Government subsidies to farmers had to be reduced by 20 per cent, 13.33 per cent in the case of developing countries. These reduction commitments did not apply to the 48 least developed countries, but they are still subject to tariffication and to providing minimum access.

The agreement provides that countries will not raise their level of protection for the agricultural sector above what they were already giving before 1993. Industrialized countries who were already affording high levels of protection can go with that protection, but developing countries cannot step up their levels. Since the Agreement was signed in 1993, the EU and the US have made few changes in their agricultural policies, claiming that they had already made most of the cuts called for in the Uruguay Round agreement. Rather, the opposite has occurred. The level of overall subsidization of agriculture in Western countries rose from US$182 billion in 1995, when the WTO was born, to US$280 billion in 1997 and US$362 billion in 1998.

The Agreement allows developing countries to place certain policies in a 'Green Box'. These are exempt from reductions, as they are deemed not to distort trade. They include spending on domestic food aid, public stockholding for food security purposes, safety-net programmes and disaster relief. More significant measures, such as import controls, cannot be placed in the box. Article 20 of the Agreement provided that it be reviewed in the year that developed countries were due to have fulfilled their obligations, that is, 2000.

The Agreement also has a 'Blue Box' under which direct government payments that are related to production-limiting programmes are exempt from reductions. But the Agreement contains a 'Peace Clause' which restricts the countervailing measures that a country can take.

All these special boxes and provisions have meant little in practice. The evidence from developing countries is that trade liberalization has led to a huge surge of imports into developing countries (but not to an increase in exports), forcing millions off their land, and to a concentration of land holdings. This hardly makes for a strong sustainable economy, or for food security (see Chapter 5).

Another Uruguay Round agreement, on the Application of Sanitary and Phytosanitary Measures, determines what human, animal, and plant health standards 'can be used to discriminate against imports ... developing countries saw strict enforcement of multilateral sanitary standards as a means to protect their exporters from the arbitrary introduction of unjustifiable standards'.[4] Some NGOs believe, however, that this could complicate the issue of market access for developing countries (see Chapter 8).

The Trade-Related Intellectual Property Rights (TRIPs) agreement, another Uruguay Round creation, grants corporations the right to protect their 'intellectual property' in all WTO countries; its rules on the patenting of life forms, especially seeds, have a direct bearing on food security (see Chapter 6).

The Uruguay Round agreement on Trade-Related Investment Measures (TRIMs) affects measures such as the assistance that governments might give to their domestic companies. Under the agreement, special treatment for domestic companies is not allowed; governments have to afford the same treatment to foreign investors. Neither can they insist that foreign investors use local labour. They cannot take measures which they believe would allow their own industries to develop and create economic linkages that might help their development effort, if that could be challenged by other countries as a restraint on their trade. National legislation that stands in the way of this principle has to be revoked.

The TRIMs agreement – which prepared the way for the OECD's notorious and ill-fated Multilateral Agreement on Investment – means that a government cannot stipulate that a foreign-owned hotel, for example, should buy locally produced foodstuffs. The hotel is free to buy all its food from abroad. There may be no link between a hotel and local farmers – the latter gain nothing from its presence. The agreement ties the hands of poor countries, making development policy subservient to trade policy.

Under the Uruguay Round agreements 'special and differential treatment' is supposed to be afforded to developing countries. In practice, however, this has proved to be of little or no value. A section on anti-dumping says, for example, that 'special regard must be given by developed country members to the special situation of developing country members'. But the dumping of foodstuffs still goes on, depressing markets for local farmers (see next chapter).

The case for free trade

The case for trade liberalization is that it will bring about the best use of resources. The theory of comparative advantage lies at the heart of the case. This maintains that all will gain when countries specialize in producing those goods and services in which they are efficient, that they can produce at lower cost than other countries. Exchanging those goods and services with other countries is a central requirement of the theory. Its advocates hold that trade liberalization leads to increased prosperity which benefits the poor as well as the rich, and that poorer countries gain more from trading than not trading.

One of the strongest claims made for trade liberalization is that it will help economic growth. David Nelson Smith, former Vice-President of Cargill, is a believer:[5]

If you are going to combat poverty you need economic growth, which needs a strong agricultural sector to create a surplus. Growth requires that resources are switched out of agriculture so that they can be used in the rest of the economy. There is a strong correlation between economic growth and being open to trade. The cure for hunger is trade. Self-sufficiency doesn't work. Isolation has led to famines. Trade liberalization is the key to economic success. If it works for industry, it works for agriculture.

Another claim is that it can provide opportunities for increased market access, and thus for improved export earnings in developing countries, which in turn will feed the hungry.

In November 1999 the Paris-based OECD published a report which suggests that the elimination of trade barriers will assist economic growth. It said that full liberalization of tariffs would led to a 3 per cent gain in world GDP. The report estimated a gain to India of 9.6 per cent, to China of 5.5 per cent and to sub-Saharan Africa of 3.7 per cent. Free trade leads to higher rates of economic growth than does protectionism, argue its advocates.

> Trade policy theory does not unambiguously suggest that protection has a negative impact on growth in developing countries. However, those countries applying more open trade regimes, together with fiscal discipline and good governance, have enjoyed higher growth rates than those implementing restrictive policies.[6]

Advocates of trade liberalization acknowledge that jobs may be lost in the process, but 'if there is a change on one farm which may be for the worse, the world as a whole is not a loser', says Simon Maxwell, director of the London-based Overseas Development Institute, because 'as economies change, people move from one sector to another; low food prices are good for industrial growth and for the creation of jobs in other places. What causes hunger to fall is what happens in the economy as a whole.'[7]

Rising agricultural productivity frees up people and resources for the development of industrial and service sectors in the economy while also building demand for their output. In a word, market-based agricultural systems are powerful engines of economic development, runs free trade theory. People displaced from their land because of trade liberalization are not seen as people who have lost their livelihoods but as 'variable factors of off-farm production', in the words of an FAO official.[8]

Free trade advocates claim that the money earned from food

exports enables people to buy more food than they could have produced themselves. This is not supported by the facts, says Indian agriculturalist Vandana Shiva:[9]

> We were told we would be able to buy more food by selling flowers than we grew for ourselves. But selling flowers destroys your food security – you can only buy a quarter of the food that you stopped producing. For every dollar earned by shrimp exports, more than ten dollars in local food security is being destroyed.

Advocates also claim that trade liberalization got a bad name in the latter years of the 1990s because of the way that developing countries opened up their markets, as they were obliged to do under the 1993 Uruguay Round agreement, while the countries of the European Union did not do the same. On the contrary, the EU hung on to its Common Agricultural Policy and did not permit the entry into European countries of many foodstuffs that developing counties wanted to sell. Advocates argue that abolishing the CAP will diminish over-production of subsidized surpluses in Europe and the dumping of cheap food in developing countries. Such dumping often has disastrous consequences for farmers in developing countries – it undercuts their prices and can force them out of business. Elimination of these surpluses will raise world food prices and encourage developing countries to export more, it is claimed, and world food production will rise as a consequence of trade liberalization. Abolish the CAP, and trade liberalization will work more evenly and eventually benefit the poor, runs the argument; abolish all barriers to trade and developing countries will gain as they will export more goods to the West.

The case against

The arguments for free trade are seductive, but especially in today's economically globalized world, dominated by transnational corporations, they are deeply flawed. Free trade no longer exists; effectively the international trading system has been captured by the corporations. And while, historically, free trade has raised the living standards of most people, it has not done this for the poorest people. It has not helped to raise the poorest out of poverty. Many of the poor have little to trade, but the theory of comparative advantage suggests that poor countries will gain if they trade and that those gains can be used to help the poor. The gains might eventually 'trickle down' to the poor.

Like 'trickle down' theory, the theory of comparative advantage is discredited. It may work if trade takes place between countries at roughly equal stages of economic development. When it takes place between wealthy countries selling industrial goods and much poorer countries selling primary products, the former are likely to gain most from the deal. This happened throughout the twentieth century when the theory was given every chance to work. But the terms on which developing countries trade turned against them; they had to export more in order to import the same amount. In pre-globalization days, trade did not benefit many of the poorest countries, let alone their poorest people. And with the coming of globalization came a new factor – the concentration of power in larger entities, in practice transnational companies, who want market power so as to dominate trade and ensure they profit the most.

Growth theory is also discredited. Growth is clearly not the same as development. Human development, the alleviation of poverty, may be helped by economic growth (although this depends on how it's measured – an increase in subsistence food output would not count in growth statistics, for example) but it depends on many other things – like freedom of choice, freedom to decide, freedom to live in dignity. By the late 1990s the free-trading, globalized economy was becoming a threat to these basic freedoms and to development itself. In some countries it was driving people from their land, giving them no choice but to drift into the cities or to work as labourers on land that was once theirs. Free trade has enslaved rather than freed them. Some developing countries – Sri Lanka is sometimes touted as an example – appear to be a success story in terms of economic growth. But this is of little comfort to the many thousands forced off their land because of trade liberalization policies (see Chapter 5).

To analyse trade only in terms of what it will do for economic growth is therefore not sufficient. The deeper questions are – who will get the benefit of the growth? Will the growth be sustainable, will it lead to sustainable development? Above all, does growth lay the basis for food security? When these questions are considered, the limits of what economic growth can achieve become glaringly apparent – the supposed benefits of growth are exposed as a false hope.

It is of course the case with liberalization that 'it is often easier to see who the losers are than who the eventual winners will be'.[9] But the chief 'eventual winners' can be spotted with little difficulty. It will be transnational corporations who will reap the gains of the economic growth that is brought about by liberalization. The rise of food imports into developing countries has forced farmers in developing countries off their land, while transnationals have become more dominant. It will be they rather than ordinary people who will reap the benefits of growth. The concentration of land holdings means that more land is likely to come under their control. For example, the corporate goal of Cargill, a major player in the food and agricultural sector, is to double in size every 5 to 7 years. It can only do that by taking over land at present farmed by local people. International conglomerates will prosper from growth while the poor stay hungry.

While there seems to be some force in the argument that a strong economy causes poverty and hunger to fall, the fact is after 20 years of intense trade liberalization in the 1980s and 1990s, hunger had not fallen. The destruction of small farmer livelihoods, and the concentration of small farms into large ones, is hardly conducive to sustainable agricultural development. Food security can hardly be built on the broken back of a devastated agricultural sector.

> Positive trade liberalization effects may eventually relieve the poor, but in the short/medium term the whole adjustment process may be more harmful than helpful. We need to know much more about this. In order to benefit, the poor need to enjoy trade-induced price reductions for consumer goods, as well as reduced input and increased output prices which they face as producers.... [T]he poor may experience increased income risks in the short run when they switch from producing subsistence-local goods to producing tradable goods. Given the imperfect working of credit markets, these risks may considerably worsen conditions for the poor.[11]

Given that growth will strengthen the hand of transnational corporations, it follows that worsening conditions for the poor are unlikely to be confined to the short-to-medium term. On the contrary, any hopes that trade liberalization will contribute to people's welfare in the long term are dashed by the reality of the kind of world that liberalization is leading to – a world of dispossessed small farmers, where transnationals own the means of production and have economic control of the lives of the poor, but have no allegiance to the countries in which they operate. In this situation, poverty is hardly likely to be alleviated, nor food security advanced. The hungry cannot rely on the long term to sort out the problems the international trading system has created for them in the short term.

In the 1980s and 1990s some developing countries made economic progress while the poorest countries stayed poor. As trade liberalization strengthens the strong, often at the expense of the weak, further liberalization may lead to a widening of the gap between developing countries. The goal of food security for all floats on such turbulent waters. Although trade liberalization may lead in some countries to higher rates of economic growth, it is also likely to lead to the marginalization of the poor and even to famine and civil unrest. Higher growth rates do not necessarily translate into food security.

Neither is the choice before governments between free trade or protectionism. There are ways in which the international trading system can be changed to work for the poor (see Chapter 9). Reasonable safeguards for the poor are likely to be needed. These should not be confused with 1930s-style protectionism.

The problem with trade policy is that it appears to dwarf all other considerations, including the health of small businesses. A government with a dominant trade policy tends to support companies that trade, and in practice these are mostly larger companies, including transnationals, rather than small enterprises. Trade liberalization policies can therefore threaten the small businesses that the poor start and run as their economic lifeline. The TRIMs agreement (see above) does not help local companies. Liberalization plunges smaller companies into the same economic stream as powerful corporations, to the inevitable detriment of the former (see Chapter 5). 'Many trade policies are not very favourable to the survival of micro enterprises,' says M. S. Swaminathan.[12]

A further charge against trade liberalization is that it has encouraged trade in products which have caused considerable environmental damage while bringing few if any benefits to local people. Intensive prawn farming in coastal areas of Asian countries is an example. Because it is capable of earning additional foreign exchange, this type of farming has been encouraged under the structural adjustment programmes of the IMF and the World Bank. Thus aid from the World Bank is helping India to develop aquaculture. Yet an investigation by India's National Environmental Engineering Research Institute found that 'damage caused to ecology and economies by the aquaculture farming is higher than the earnings from the sale of coastal aquaculture produce'.[13] Such damage is hardly conducive to food security. Prawn farming, as currently practised in India and Bangladesh, is disastrous for local communities. Yet the World Bank, a major international aid agency, is using aid funds to finance this 'disaster' for the poor.

Abolishing the EU's Common Agricultural Policy would be helpful to developing countries. Above all it would end or severely reduce food dumping (see next chapter), and would give developing countries greater access for their foodstuffs to a large market. Of course, in theory abolishing *all* barriers to trade would help developing country exports. But universal abolition would not solve some of the chief problems associated with trade liberalization – the takeover of land, for example, by large entities, and the dominant role of transnational corporations in trade.

Export-dominated trade policies

In the 1980s and 1990s, a number of developing countries pursued policies dominated by international trade. The need to increase exports and to earn more foreign exchange – often to pay off foreign debts – was frequently met, however, at the expense of agricultural policies and food security, worsening the plight of the hungry. Latin America provides an example.

A huge growth in the export of fruit, vegetables and flowers from Latin America to the United States has occurred over the last twenty years. Much of Latin America's best farmland is now growing not just traditional export crops, such as coffee, banana, sugar and cotton, but also products for export such as mangoes, soya beans and roses. These non-traditional crops can fetch high prices. While world grain prices range from US$75 to US$175 a tonne, a tonne of fresh fruit and vegetables can fetch US$500, for example. For those in control, the business is profitable. But the people in control are large landowners, wealthy investors and foreign companies. Larger businesses have accumulated land in agro-export crops while poorer farmers have been squeezed out of the market and pushed onto marginal land.

The trade has frequently been at the expense of food for local people and has come 'at a cost in workers' health, inequitable distribution of economic benefits, and environmental degradation in many of the exporting countries'.[14] In 1980, Chile, for example, exported about the same amount of beans, an important staple, as it grew for local consumption. But by the early 1990s the quantity of beans exported was almost three times higher – 55,000 tonnes a year, compared with 20,000 tonnes grown for local consumption.

Between 1989 and 1993 the area in Chile under basic food crops fell by nearly 30 per cent, from 1.2 to 0.86 million hectares. Fruit, flowers and other crops destined for the export market had replaced beans, wheat and other staple foods. Large-scale fruit producers bought out small farmers who could not afford to invest in the new crops and this 'has changed the face of the country's agriculture and embittered many small farmers'.[15]

Brazil's big new export earner was soya beans. In 1970, soya beans grew on 1.4 million hectares of land; by 1988, this crop was growing on 10.5 million hectares. Argentina followed Brazil's example. The area under soya beans has risen, since the early 1970s, from 10,000 hectares to 5 million hectares. Mexico and other Central American countries have greatly increased their export of vegetables to the United States.

Government support for farmers to help them sustain the production of food staples has fallen dramatically in many countries on the continent. Governments are now more interested in how they can use land for export crops; scientists have been switched to work on these crops. This is reflected in research spending. In the 1980s, around 90 per cent of the money that Latin American countries spent on agricultural research went on food crops, especially beans. There has now been an almost total change in emphasis.

Only about 20 per cent of agricultural research spending is devoted to food crops, while 80 per cent is going to export crops. These are now the priorities of Latin American countries. Land is not seen, primarily, as the place on which to grow food for local people, but as something from which a country can earn more foreign exchange. In some countries on the continent, research into small farmer problems has been abandoned completely. 'In the absence of adequate technical assistance to sustain the production of food staples, small farmers have been forced into growing export crops,' says Francisco Morales of the Colombia-based International Centre for Tropical Agriculture.[16]

Small-scale farmers and consumers in Latin American are paying the price of this drastic shift to export agriculture. In towns and cities across the continent, beans are now frequently scarce as land which once grew beans now grows vegetables for export. Beans contribute around 30 per cent of the protein consumed by the continent's 200 million low-income families. Most bean farmers are now trying to grow vegetables for export and devoting less of their land (often already small) to beans for their own use. Millions of the poor have seen their food security decline as a result of this trade.

The export of flowers also took off in a number of African countries in the late 1990s, again raising questions about the impact on food security. In Kenya, for example, there has been a big expansion in horticulture, producing flowers for export, on land around Lake Naivasha that was previously ranching land and small farms. Kenya is already short of land for producing food, and there are conflicts between expanding horticultural schemes and Maasai cattle owners, who claim the land surrounding Lake Naivasha is theirs.

Irrigation systems used by the flower industry make big demands on local water sources. Estimates suggest that an additional 15 cm of water is being extracted each year from Lake Naivasha by the flower growers. This inevitably means that less water is available for food crop farmers. Horticulture cannot continue to expand in Kenya without intensifying conflicts over land and water.

Conclusion

The World Food Summit commitment of governments was modest enough. Hunger needs to be abolished, not halved. But even this modest commitment will not be fulfilled unless governments fully incorporate food security into world trade negotiations and agreements.

The world has experienced an era of trade-dominated food and agricultural policies. Land is being used for growing food for export rather than food for local people. People abroad can afford to buy that food, whereas people in the producing country don't have that purchasing power. The international trade system has not contributed to food security; instead it has emerged as an obstacle. Rather than another era of trade-dominated policies and trade liberalization, the world needs to balance trade with the interests of domestic food production, and to ensure that trade gives producers a decent return and contributes to food security.

Trade can only be 'a key element' in achieving food security if it is trade which is democratic, free from corporate control, and helpful rather than a hindrance to the poor. Policy makers need to switch the emphasis from free trade to a system which enables the poor to escape from poverty and helps to feed the hungry.

CHAPTER 4

INTERNATIONAL ORGANIZATIONS
AND POLICIES

The policies of a number of international organizations have an important influence on trade and food security. The key players are discussed below.

The World Bank and the International Monetary Fund

Trade liberalization is a central part of the structural adjustment programmes (SAPs) that the World Bank and the International Monetary Fund insist that developing countries implement if they want aid, debt relief and investment. The World Bank and the IMF are Washington-based sister organizations, set up in 1945 following a conference at Bretton Woods, USA. The Bank's role is to fund projects in developing countries, while traditionally the Fund has assisted with balance of payments problems. In practice, as economist John Maynard Keynes is reputed to have said, the World Bank is a fund and the IMF is a bank.

SAPs were introduced by the Bank and the Fund in 1980 when many developing countries were in deep recession, caused partly by factors outside their control. By the late 1990s, over 80 developing countries had implemented or were implementing these programmes. A typical SAP requires a government to liberalize trade, reduce spending on social programmes such as health care and education, eliminate food subsidies and increase the prices they pay to growers of crops for the export market. SAPs are supposed to lead to economic recovery, long-term growth and stability. But their record is dismal. SAPs have led to hunger for the poor and have even failed when measured against the criteria of the Fund and the Bank. In most countries, they have not led to the higher economic growth they were supposed to be all about. And they have not led to development; few people have seen any benefits.

SAPs have concentrated on domestic changes in developing countries, but ignored the international changes needed if these countries were to have a chance of recovery. Crucially, they ignore the need for improved trading arrangements for crops that are exported. And the policy of paying producers higher prices for export crops has led to their expansion at the expense of food crops; food output has often declined as a result. Farmers in Zimbabwe, for example, have been encouraged to replace maize with tobacco. SAPs have also caused governments to reduce their support for small farmers, which again has lowered food output. This has happened in some of the most famine-prone countries, such as Ethiopia.

The cumulative effect of trade liberalization, reduction in food subsidies, higher food prices and (often) lower wages is that in both urban and rural areas poorer households cannot afford to buy as much food as before. Access to food by vulnerable households has especially become more difficult.

A UN Economic Commission for Africa report said that SAPs

> have not succeeded in addressing the real issues and in many cases have even failed to address and deal with the real causes behind the African crisis. Further, the programmes generally failed to capture the political, social, cultural and economic realities of African countries.

Drastic budgetary reductions, it says, 'undermine the human condition ... and the future potential for development'.

Indiscriminate promotion of export crops undermines food production and self-sufficiency, the report points out, while 'import liberalization leads to greater and more entrenched external dependence ... [and] jeopardises national priorities such as food self-sufficiency'. The withdrawal or reduction of support for farmers, under SAPs, has hit the poorest farmers the hardest, and led to a huge increase in the number of people who have migrated into urban areas (see next chapter.)

Higher prices for export crops make it more attractive for transnational corporations and larger, more prosperous farmers to buy land. Such entities are in a favourable position – they can obtain credit from the banks, for example, that peasant farmers often cannot get. If smaller farmers cannot survive, their land will probably be bought by larger farmers or transnationals and used to grow crops for export.

In some countries, Bolivia for example, the maxim that the land goes to the people who work it is being challenged. In Sri Lanka, 'the poor majority of the mainly rural people are increasingly being pushed out of their livelihoods in agriculture', says Sarath Fernando of the country's Movement for National Land and Agricultural Reform; 'trade liberalization is destroying millions of livelihoods; structural adjustment policies are making the country more dependent [and] lead to widespread malnutrition, women skipping meals and feeling faint in the fields, children passing out in school assembly'.[1]

When charges for health and education are imposed under SAPs, it is women and girls who are less likely to go to school or to a clinic for health care. When money and food are short, it is more likely to be women and girls who get less to eat than men and boys.

At the IMF–World Bank annual meeting in September 1999, changes were announced to the IMF's remit. The fund will in future focus on poverty reduction rather than stabilization and growth. This seems a welcome change. But while it gives developing countries the opportunity to seize the initiative, it does not necessarily translate into good news for the poor. In many cases the requirements of World Bank–IMF SAPs are far harsher than is required under WTO regulations, and developing countries bear obligations which go beyond their commitments under the WTO.

The World Trade Organization

While the World Bank and the IMF began the contemporary process of trade liberalization, it is the Geneva-based WTO that makes the rules. In a world dominated by trade, it is the WTO that dominates trade. With 137 member countries (in mid-2000) the WTO has the task of enforcing the 1993 Uruguay Round agreements – the Agreement on Agriculture, the General Agreement on Services, and the agreements on TRIPs and TRIMs. WTO rules are prolific, running into thousands of pages. This has confirmed the view that the rules are more consistent with corporate-managed rather than 'free' trade (see Chapter 5).

The WTO presents itself as a forum for members to negotiate over trade liberalization. In practice the organization is a trade liberalization juggernaut which has been ceded enormous power by its members. It uses that position to further the cause of liberalization, to the chief benefit of those who stand to gain most: in practice, the transnational corporations. The Organization's first director-general, Renato Ruggiero, said in 1998 that

> we stand at the very beginning of a whole new phase of international-ism. We are living through a time of deep and rapid transition towards a very different world. [We have] an opportunity to reaffirm our political will to move towards a better system of global governance ... shaping the institutions of an increasingly borderless economy. The great promise of the new global age demands nothing else.[2]

The vision is therefore one of a borderless world economy, of global governance, based on free trade.

The WTO is both a forum and a judge, exercising considerable and direct power through its disputes settlement mechanism. This lies at the heart of the organization. The mechanism has been used mainly by the developed countries – there have been about 150 cases, of which the US has initiated about 50 and the developing countries, together, about 40.

A panel consisting of three people normally adjudicates on a dispute. The panelists are not necessarily lawyers but their judgements have to be obeyed on pain of sanctions, even if they contradict national laws. The panels invariably uphold the strict letter of free trade. 'So far, its pronouncements have been consistent with the need to remain focused on trade and the needs of trade.'[3] Pronouncements have also tended to benefit transnational companies. On bananas, a WTO panel has ruled for the US and Latin American countries against special treatment for Caribbean banana growers, leading the Prime Minister of Dominica, Mr Edison James, to speak of the 'blind and insensitive application of WTO rules'.[4] It is the large banana companies that will benefit.

The free trade philosophy of the WTO has had a powerful influence on other international negotiations. The OECD's proposed Multilateral Agreement on Investment was based on the notion that free trade is paramount. The MAI was essentially a development of the Uruguay Round TRIMs agreement. Negotiations from September 1998 between the European Union and African, Caribbean and Pacific countries on a new trade-and-aid 'Lomé Convention' were heavily influenced by WTO philosophy. The EU insisted that a new agreement had to conform with WTO rules.

Food security is defined by the WTO as a 'concept which discourages opening up the domestic market to foreign agricultural produce, on the principle that a country must be as self-sufficient as possible for its basic dietary needs'.[5] This definition is a long way from the internationally accepted definition of food security (see last chapter) and seems calculated to try to prejudice opinion against the concept. The definition discloses a WTO bias against food security, despite the organization's claim to be neutral.

The WTO's Agreement on Agriculture covers market access, export subsidies, and domestic support for agriculture (see Chapter 3). Non-trade concerns, including food security, are mentioned in the Agreement's preamble. Developing countries can provide investment subsidies, input subsidies to low-income or resource-poor producers, and support to encourage diversification from illegal narcotic crop cultivation as long as they do not exceed 1992 levels. Negative effects of the Uruguay Round are foreseen.

Commitments under the reform programme should be made in an equitable way among all members, having regard to non-trade concerns, including food security and the need to protect the environment, having regard to the agreement that special and differential treatment to developing countries is an integral element of the negotiations, and taking into account the possible negative effects of the implementation of the reform programme on least developed and net food-importing countries.

A Committee on Agriculture was set up under the Agreement to oversee its implementation.

Under the Agreement, two sets of rules have been enforced, says Rashid Kaukab of the South Centre:

one for those who were responsible for distorting the market through tariff and non-tariff barriers and high domestic and export subsidies. They have been allowed to continue to do so with only minor adjustments. The second set of rules is for those, including developing countries, who were not indulging in such practices. Now they are legally prohibited to do so.[6]

In practice it is Western countries, not developing countries, that have received special treatment.

The 'special' treatment that developing countries were supposed to receive on processed products, including foodstuffs, is again negative. A system of tariff escalation means that higher tariffs are placed against their processed goods; the greater the processing, the higher the tariff. This hinders processing in developing countries. The Uruguay Round agreement did nothing to lower most of these barriers.

Article 20 of the Agreement on Agriculture provides for its review in the year that developed countries are required to have fulfilled their obligations, that is, 2000. This is a part of the Uruguay Round's 'built-in' agenda, of which services TRIPs and TRIMs are also part. Even before the Seattle meeting, WTO member countries had agreed to start negotiations on agriculture by January 2000 'with the aim of achieving substantial progressive reductions in support and protection'.[7]

Transnational corporations have a powerful influence on the WTO's agenda. While it is ministers and their officials who conduct business at WTO meetings, representatives from major corporations are often there to lobby for decisions which help their business, and they may even be part of the official delegation. 'The enormous role TNCs can play in a nation's economy can make their host government a very accommodating and attentive audience; the corporations have much more access to WTO decision makers than citizens' groups and NGOs'[8] (see also Chapter 1).

Transnationals can even be powerful enough to turn WTO member applications to their own advantage – urging, for example, that a developing country wanting to join the WTO should not be allowed in unless it does more to liberalize its economy. A corporation that is barred from selling its goods to an aspiring WTO member country may urge that it lifts the ban on those goods before it can join. What is clear is that lobbying of this kind has secured new international trade rules that are intended to create 'a world order moulded in the image of multinationals'.[9]

The requirements of countries under the WTO cannot be separated from obligations to other international bodies. While, under WTO rules, developing countries are allowed to protect their farmers by placing tariffs on agricultural imports, the structural adjustment programmes of the World Bank and the IMF may not permit this.

International trade rules, overseen by the WTO, are based on the principle of non-discrimination – countries are not allowed to discriminate in favour of domestic companies to the detriment of foreign companies (see Chapter 8). The rules take precedence over national interests, such as socioeconomic impacts and environmental considerations, and even legislation.

> The agreements and dispute settlements at the WTO make clear that free trade is given higher priority than the welfare of citizens, consumers or the environment. But liberalization goes further, ensuring that every aspect of society is organized in a way which promotes the pursuit of corporate profit. Governments are no longer expected to govern in the interests of their citizens, their prime task is the pursuit of free market economic growth.[10]

WTO rules also limit the right of member countries to restrict the production and trade of genetically modified foods, and could stop them from introducing mandatory labelling of these foods (see Chapter 6). They also limit the right of countries to design their own intellectual property legislation (see Chapter 7).

A human right

The WTO is also being challenged on human rights grounds. Food is a human right, as defined in the United Nations charter. 'What about the human rights of people suffering malnutrition and increasing poverty, of farmers losing their land? There are very important human rights being violated here,' says Sarath Fernando.[11]

'Anything, any institution, that negates people's right to food needs to be challenged,' believes the New York-based People's Decade for Human Rights Education (PDHRE). The WTO is in this category, it believes. 'The promotion and protection of human rights and funda-mental freedoms is the first responsibility of governments,' it says, and 'the WTO has no immunity from human rights'. PDHRE claims that the WTO is a United Nations charter-based organization and must adhere to the Universal Declaration of Human Rights.

The WTO must mainstream human rights principles and goals throughout the organization and incorporate them in policy formula-tion, implementation and review. It must admit the primacy of inter-national human rights law over its trade rules and agreements. It must counter fears that its trade sanction powers will lead to human rights protectionism by ceding enforcement authority to fully empowered United Nations human rights bodies and machinery.[12]

'The World Trade Organization stands at a crossroads,' says PDHRE:

it must choose whether international trade rules will actively promote a fairer, more sustainable world .... [T]he WTO has so far refused to acknowledge its human rights obligations under international law or examine the human rights dimensions of international trade policy. Human rights are not for trading away.

Can the WTO survive? 'No international agreement can survive if it is not people-friendly,' says Devinder Sharma of India.

The WTO is being orchestrated by the bureaucrats and the neoclassic economists for the benefit of the multinational companies and the corporate world. We are in an era when all governments, without exception, have begun to represent only the vested interests of the industry. In the bargain, the poor and hungry are being further marginalized .... [A]s a placard at the protests in the streets [of Seattle] read: WTO is a Wrong Trade Organization.[13]

'The more power the WTO gets to itself, Ralph Nader believes, 'the more its rules are enforced, the more opposition it's going to generate to defeat it and to replace it with a renegotiated pull-up trade agreement, instead of what it is now a pull-down trade agreement in terms of world standards.'[14] Developing countries clearly want changes in the WTO. 'Special and differential treatment for developing countries should constitute an integral part of the negotiations in order to take fully into account the development and food security needs of developing countries,' said a statement by African countries in Seattle. 'The WTO should be given a much narrower trade-orientated remit. It should be confined to trade issues and trade issues only,' believes Murasoli Maran, India's Minister of Commerce.[15] And the WTO is likely to see further calls for changes in the way it operates and for checks on its power. The outcome of the Biosafety Protocol, (see Chapter 7) appears to be one such check.

United Nations bodies

The UN Conference on Trade and Development (UNCTAD)

UNCTAD is an international trade and development organization that commands wide respect among developing countries. Western countries, on the other hand, have effectively disabled it. Set up in 1964, UNCTAD's initial brief was to help developing countries to reverse their declining terms of trade and to link trade with development. It decided to hold a major meeting every four years and to focus on changing the rules of international trade.

In its early years, UNCTAD launched a number of ambitious programmes, the most significant the idea of an Integrated Programme
for Commodities (IPC) at UNCTAD IV in Nairobi in 1976. This
envisaged the negotiation of 18 specific commodity agreements that
would give producers a fair return and consumers a guaranteed price.
UNCTAD IV agreed that negotiations take place on a US$6 billion
common fund to finance these agreements. The fund would lend
commodity agreements money to finance price stabilization methods,
such as buffer stocks, to regulate prices when they either fell below or
climbed too far above certain negotiated price targets.

Western countries went along with the IPC idea but without any
enthusiasm. In the next four years, however, the negotiation of
commodity agreements ran into problems, with many failing to even
start; the common fund was scaled down from US$6 billion to US$750
million. The heart had been torn from the IPC idea. UNCTAD has
never effectively recovered from this setback.

During UNCTAD VIII, in 1992, Western countries insisted that
UNCTAD's functions be limited to 'analysis, consensus building on
some trade related issues and technical assistance'. In this limited role,
UNCTAD has still managed to perform some useful tasks for the South,
not least in helping developing countries with trade negotiations.

In its 1998 report, UNCTAD warned that developing countries
need to be cautious before choosing to increase dependence on world
markets for food supplies when a major part of the staple diet is food
that is not traded internationally.[16] Again, its secretary-general, Rubens
Ricupero, has articulated concerns of developing countries. In 1999,
he cautioned that the Seattle ministerial meeting provided an opportunity for the international community 'to concentrate not only on
removing barriers to trade and investment ... but also on how to
improve the rules governing trade to ensure that they meet the needs
of all countries, especially those inadequately equipped to cope with a
more competitive global economy'. He said that a 'positive trade
agenda' is needed, including an exploration of 'constructive remedies
before applying anti-dumping duties to developing countries exports'.[17]

There is 'nothing wrong with trade liberalization', believes
Ricupero, but it has to be achieved in 'a gradual, equitable and balanced

way ... developing countries need to protect their policy autonomy'. He points out that 'Despite all the promises regarding the liberalization of trade, the reality has been very disappointing.' And he makes it clear that the legitimacy of the WTO, as of any international organization, depends on the universality of membership, participatory decision making and fair sharing of the benefits of the system.

UNCTAD has pointed out that discrimination, in the form of tariff peaks (high tariffs) and escalating tariffs, persists against exports from developing countries that are viewed as sensitive by developed countries. It pointed out that the European Union, for example, applies a 73 per cent tariff on cane sugar from developing countries, 84 per cent on maize and 65 per cent on wheat. It said that the removal of such high tariffs should be given priority if trade liberalization was to have credibility and widespread political support.[18]

UNCTAD could lead the way in forging a 'New Deal' for agriculture in developing countries, says Walden Bello:

> the emphasis would not be the integration of agriculture into world trade but the integration of trade into a development strategy that will put the emphasis on raising incomes and employment in the agricultural sector, achieving food security through a significant degree of food self-sufficiency, and promoting ecologically sustainable production.... [UNCTAD] should challenge the role of the WTO as the ultimate arbiter of trade and development issues ... putting forward an arrangement where trade, development, and environment issues must be formulated and interpreted by a wider body of global organizations.[19]

UNCTAD X, held in Bangkok in February 2000, though styled 'a world parliament on globalization', offered more rhetoric than substance.

> Key players in the globalization debate, i.e. Moore, Camdessus, Wolfenson (WTO, IMF and World Bank heads respectively), stressed globalization benefiting the poorest, development must be more inclusive, etc. What is lacking is concrete commitment; there was no clear sense of how this has to be done.[20]

UNCTAD X ended with a declaration which says that new trade talks should take the development dimension into account.

Food and Agriculture Organization (FAO)

Trade is a key element in achieving world food security, believes the FAO, the UN's largest specialized agency.

> Trade generates effective utilisation of resources and stimulates economic growth which is critical to improving food security. Trade allows food consumption to exceed food production, helps to reduce production and consumption fluctuations and relieves part of the burden of stock-holding. It has a major bearing on access to food through its positive effect on economic growth, income and employment. [21]

The FAO says that developing countries will

> require assistance in building and strengthening their capacities to analyse policy options, monitor developments in the world trading system, integrate trade issues in domestic policy formulation and assess the relationship between the multilateral trading systems and their commitments to regional trading arrangements. [22]

It points to synergies between the FAO and the WTO in the area of trade, with FAO being the principal source of scientific expertise on a range of environmental matters, including biodiversity.

The FAO believes that 'for some commodities, tariff escalation constitutes probably one of the major constraints to vertical diversification of their agricultural exports'. [23] Tariff escalation occurs when tariffs rise with stages of processing and can hinder the attempts of developing countries to develop food processing industries.

In September 1999, the FAO published a paper showing the effects of trade liberalization on 16 developing countries (see next chapter). It has avoided a direct clash with the WTO, despite growing evidence of the threat of trade liberalization to food security.

UN Development Programme

The UNDP's 1999 *Human Development Report* describes the WTO as 'far from adequate, given the long-term priorities for improving the situation in developing countries'. It suggests that the mandate of the WTO 'needs to be expanded to give it anti-monopoly functions over the activities of multinational corporations'. [24] This is, however, to show no understanding of the close relationship that exists between the corporations and the WTO, and the larger member governments of the WTO.

The European Union

The EU's Common Agricultural Policy is one of the world's most protectionist devices and has a detrimental impact on food security in developing countries. The 15 EU countries spend US$42 billion a year subsidizing their farmers through this policy, against the estimated US$30 billion that they give in development aid for all purposes, inevitably putting pressure on the money they have available to meet their international commitments to reduce poverty. The CAP has been little affected by the Uruguay Round agreement.

The CAP's support to farmers takes the form of direct payments, intervention prices, storage facilities for surplus production and export subsidies. These measures have stabilized food prices in the EU but have transferred the fluctuations that would have taken place in this market onto the world market. Such fluctuations have created insecurity and difficult production conditions for developing countries. Estimates suggest that dismantling the CAP could diminish the fluctuations by between 25 and 50 per cent.

The CAP's export subsidies mean that EU produce competes with the produce of farmers in developing countries. Its import barriers deprive farmers in developing countries of export possibilities. The CAP means that farmers in the EU overproduce, which may lead to lower world food prices. In the short term this can benefit the net-food-importing countries; it may also benefit urban dwellers and the landless, but it does so at a cost to agriculture.

The Agreement on Agriculture has not obliged the EU to change the CAP. The EU is able to claim that it had made the required changes before 1995 (the CAP was last reformed in 1992, and the Agreement's 'reference' period for the reductions was backdated). Developed countries have exploited the ambiguous nature of commitments in the Agreement. Under its Agenda 2000 proposals for reforming the CAP the EU floated plans to cut intervention (minimum) prices to its farmers by 20 per cent on grain, 30 per cent on beef, and 15 per cent on dairy products. EU government leaders scaled these down in March 1999, although without making any significant reforms in the CAP.

If the policy is eventually reformed and the EU produces less food, then less is likely be dumped in developing countries and more will need to be imported into the EU. Governments of developing countries are pressing for greater access to EU markets (see last chapter). Significant reforms in the CAP may be slow. While the review of the Agreement on Agriculture may accept further liberalization, 'to be implemented over the period 2006–2010 ... despite increasing liberalization in agricultural markets, the CAP will not have been eliminated. It will continue to offer EU producers significant levels of border protection and some domestic support.'[25] Only budgetary pressures on EU governments are likely to bring significant reforms. While the EU preaches free trade, the CAP shows that it does not practise what is preaches. 'You can't preach the pure water of free markets when you drink subsidized wine and milk,' points out WTO Director-General Mike Moore.[26]

The CAP is not just costly for EU taxpayers and Third World farmers but also unjust to many farmers in the EU. Three-quarters of CAP subsidies go to a quarter of EU farmers – the larger farmers. Tens of thousands of small farmers in the EU have gone out of business in recent years. The CAP also appears to be inconsistent with the EU's obligations under the Maastricht treaty, which requires that policies should be consistent with poverty alleviation.

Food dumping

The CAP has led to the overproduction of a wide range of agricultural products which are dumped (sold below the cost of production) in developing countries. Cereals, beef, pork, milk, butter, tomatoes, sunflower oil and sugar are among the products. For farmers in developing countries, dumping can have disastrous consequences in both the short and long terms. It undercuts their prices and can force them out of business. Consumers may gain in the short term, but should countries that dump food decide to end the practice, and the supply of cheap food to developing countries dries up, local agriculture is in a weaker position to fill the gap. Even part-reliance on dumped food is not consistent with a sound food security strategy.

Dumping is at least partly responsible for developing countries becoming more dependent on the EU in food. Thirty years ago, sub-Saharan Africa was self-sufficient in basic food staples. Imports of wheat into the region have tripled in this time, while local production has declined.

Southern African (especially South Africa and Namibia) has been badly affected by the dumping of beef and tomatoes by EU countries. Often the price at which the EU products are sold in Southern Africa bears no relationship to the cost of production in Europe. EU beef, for example, has sold in Southern Africa for about 30 pence a kilo. It costs EU farmers about £1 a kilo to produce it. 'At the peak of the trade, this subsidized beef accounted for 70 per cent of all the meat going into cans in Southern Africa,' according to Paul Goodison, of the European Research Office.[27] Namibia's canning industry has been affected:

> Namibia puts beef into cans and exports it to the Southern African region. The Namibian canning plant found that cheap EU beef was being used by other canners in the region to such an extent that it could no longer afford to buy beef locally to put into cans. The whole economics of canning beef was transformed by the EU subsidized beef exports. All this can have profound consequences; it can lead to the loss of thousands of jobs. And it's a coincidental, not an intended consequence of the CAP.

South Africa's fruit canning industry has been

> extremely hard-hit by the distortion effects of the CAP. Access to the EU market for South Africa's goods has been restricted, but subsidized European exports are flooding into the country. The fruit canning industry had become internationally competitive, with 90 per cent of its production exported. But the industry has come under severe pressure. South Africa dismantled its subsidy scheme but the EU retains CAP. In 1996, the CAP's assistance to Europe's fruit and vegetable producers totalled £450 million of which about £260

million went to tomato producers. The EU imposes tariffs of between 10.7 per cent and 23 per cent on South African canned produce.

Article 15 of the Uruguay Round's anti-dumping agreement says that 'special regard must be given by developed country members to the special situation of developing country members'. In spite of this, however, dumping goes on. 'Grain companies consistently pay US farmers less than the cost of production for their crops – the food is then sold on the international market at below the US price.'[28]

For a developing country to prove that dumping is causing harm can be difficult and costly. Anti-dumping proceedings at the WTO are like the Ritz Hotel – open to all. It is therefore rare for developing countries to challenge a developed country. By contrast, developed countries frequently invoke anti-dumping measures against developing countries.

Conclusion

The world does not have an international organization which is capable of balancing the food needs of the poor with the trading imperative of governments and corporations. Western governments do not recognize the need for such a body. Just possibly, with very substantial reforms, the World Trade Organization could play that role. Another option is to take agriculture out of WTO rules.

CHAPTER 5

TRADE LIBERALIZATION AND FOOD SECURITY: THE EVIDENCE

There is overwhelming recent evidence that trade liberalization is leading to a huge increase in food imports into developing countries, damaging the livelihoods of small-scale farmers and not helping to achieve food security. What follows draws on material published in either 1999 or 2000, and on interviews conducted in late 1999.

The FAO finds a 'surge of imports'

A UN Food and Agriculture Organization study published in September 1999 looked at the experience of 16 developing countries in implementing the Uruguay Round Agreement on Agriculture. The study finds that the Agreement has led to a surge of food imports into developing countries but not to an increase in their exports. This is forcing local farmers out of business and into the urban areas, and is leading to a concentration of farm holdings into larger entities.

The countries studied were Bangladesh, Botswana, Brazil, Egypt, Fiji, Guyana, India, Jamaica, Kenya, Morocco, Pakistan, Peru,

Senegal, Sri Lanka, Tanzania and Thailand. Between these countries
the study finds

> a remarkably similar experience with import surges in particular
> products in the post-Uuguay period. These were dairy products
> (mostly milk powder) and meat products (mainly poultry). Some
> regions, notably the small island states of the Caribbean and the South
> Pacific, seemed to be facing difficulties coping with import surges of
> these products, with detrimental effects on competing domestic
> sectors.[1]

Under the Agreement on Agriculture, 12 of the 16 countries had
reduced domestic support for their farmers. While their imports of
food have increased, 'these countries were not able to raise their
exports. Significant supply-side constraints prevented the countries
studied from taking advantage of increased global market access,' the
study says. The findings were described by an FAO official as

> contrary to what was expected. Developing countries had a lot of
> expectations (in terms of increasing their exports) from the Uruguay
> Round agreement. Many of their farmers are now finding it very
> difficult to cope with the surge in imports of basic foodstuffs.[2]

On Egypt, the study says, 'the experience with trade has not been
favourable. Imports have risen much faster than exports.' Kenya 'has
experienced negative impacts from market liberalization in the production of cotton'. Thailand was the only country studied to increase
its food exports. Jamaica's 'agricultural imports have increased significantly since the liberalization process began'. In Guyana, imports of
food and live animals almost doubled between 1994 and 1998.

> There is the fear that without adequate market protection, accompa-
> nied by agricultural development programmes, many commodities
> that have historically been produced domestically (e.g. milk, poultry,
> fruit, juice, beans, peas, cabbage and carrot) will be imported and the
> domestic diet will increasingly shift towards greater dependence on
> imported food products.

In the dairy sector of Brazil, 'farm size is increasing ... large-scale industrial processing firms are moving in (e.g. Nestlé, Parmalat) and traditional cooperatives are failing'. In maize and soya beans, farms in Brazil 'are being consolidated ... by contrast, wheat, rice and cotton sectors are declining'.

One of the case studies, on Sri Lanka, highlighted the displacement of people from rural areas:

> Food imports have witnessed a significant increase since 1996 ... the surge in imports was also followed by a decline in domestic production in a number of food products, resulting in a clear drop in rural employment. It was reported that a loss of 300,000 jobs occurred following the recent drop in the production of onions and potatoes ... further flexibility in support in the short to medium term is considered necessary to sustain agricultural development and food security.

Of the overall impact on the 16 countries, the study says that

> a common reported concern was with a general trend towards the concentration of farms, in a wide cross-section of countries. While this led to increased productivity and competitiveness with positive results, in the virtual absence of safety nets the process also marginalized small producers and added to unemployment and poverty.

Apart from the Sri Lankan evidence, no figures were given on the displacement of people. At a conservative estimate, between 20 to 30 million people in developing countries have been driven from their land because of trade liberalization in recent years. Small farmers, and also people who process small-farmer produce, have had their food security impaled on the railings of trade liberalization.

Rural poor suffer, say NGOs

Non-governmental organizations related to Brussels-based APRODEV (the Association of World Council of Churches-related Development Organizations in Europe) published findings on trade and food security in April 1999, following a conference on the issues attended by representatives of 57 civil society organizations. Thirty-six case studies from organizations in Africa, Asia and Latin America were presented. It was significant that the papers all revealed a common problem – that trade liberalization has worsened the food security of the rural poor in developing countries.[3]

The studies show that trade liberalization means more imports and more priority for crops for export; that it often reduces the priority that countries give to their food crop sector; that it concentrates power in the hands of transnationals; and that it is taking the world away from, rather than towards, the goal of food for all.

Many of the studies considered not just the effects of the Uruguay Round agreement, but the 20 years of experience that countries have had with liberalization following the imposition of structural adjustment programmes in the early 1980s. SAPs typically require governments to remove barriers to exports and imports. These programmes assumed that liberalized agricultural trade would increase food output and lead to a better deal for farmers. For food–crop farmers, at least, this has proved to be an illusion, as several of the studies show.

Trade liberalization was found to have a 'built–in' bias towards larger food producers, such as absentee landlords and transnationals, at the expense of smaller producers. SAPs have lessened the role of the state and reduced the support it gives to small farmers, while creating an economic environment favourable to the corporations. The transnationals are more interested in export crops than food crops, in lucrative foreign markets than in meeting local food needs.

A number of the studies show how SAPs have led to increased competition for land between export and food crops. With government incentives, export crops have won the battle. Exporters have gained, but the poor have suffered. The result of SAPs is that many low–income families are eating fewer meals each day and the quality of the food they are eating has declined. No longer do they expect nutritious food, but any food they can get. The studies also show how liberalization of food imports has caused an increase in food dumping in local markets to the detriment of local farmers.

The study of *Ghana* found that food imports, in the wake of SAPs,

> have demoralized the small–scale farmers. Having produced maize, rice, soya beans, rabbits, sheep and goats, these farmers cannot obtain

economic prices for them, even in village markets. Their produce cannot compete with imported maize, rice, soya beans, chicken and turkey. Smallholder incomes have fallen and malnutrition among the rural poor has risen.

It found that trade liberalization has led to the government giving priority to export crops, rather than to the food crop sector, and to food imports rather than to the encouragement of domestic food crop production. And women farmers, it says, are bearing the brunt of this.

It was assumed that the SAP and trade liberalization in *Tanzania* would improve agricultural production and lead to better prices and prompt payment for farmers' crops. This has not happened. The overall impact on food security of the liberalization of agricultural trade is

profoundly negative. Farmer incomes are declining and, at the same time, school and medical fees have been reintroduced under the SAP. Farmers have to part with some of the little money they earn, and have less to meet farming costs and to buy food in times of shortage. Food insecurity has thus increased.

For *Kenya*, trade liberalization has led to an increase of food imports into the country and caused food dumping in local markets, hitting the country's own farmers; liberalization has also led to an increase in the prices of farm inputs, putting them beyond the reach of most small farmers. 'Persistent food deficits, decreased incomes, families eating fewer meals each day, poor infrastructure, poor medical services, increased alcoholism, hooliganism and loss of any reasonable protection for farmers, are now characteristic of rural life,' says the study.

A study of *Benin* shows how land for food production has to compete with cotton production. Following government incentives, land under cotton has increased, and also cotton exports. But the food security of the poor has been undermined.

Trade liberalization has opened up *Bolivia* to imports and threatens to saturate the domestic market with products that have a detrimental effect on locally produced goods. Liberalization has caused the prices of local produce to plummet, whereas those of imports have risen and become unaffordable.

A study of rubber in Kerala, *India,* found that the government had encouraged farmers to grow more rubber for export; a huge increase in land under the crop has taken place. Under trade liberalization, the government has opened the import doors – this led has to the ruination of the small and marginal farmers the government had previously encouraged. As a result, the sustenance of the people in Kerala, a state which has so far avoided famine, is now in jeopardy.

India's liberalization policies focused on export growth and encouraged cotton exports and expansion. In the Wanangal district of Andhra Pradesh, the switch to cotton between 1986 and 1997 replaced traditional food crops such as jowar and green gram. From an annual average of 35,000 tonnes in the 1980s, raw cotton exports rose dramatically to 374,000 tonnes in 1990–1. Huge rises in the price of cotton made it an attractive crop for farmers. But high returns from cotton did not last long for farmers who could not afford the rising cost of inputs; these put smaller farmers, especially, under severe financial pressure. 'The economic reforms have not reduced the vulnerability of the farming community, especially the poorer segments. The resulting accumulated debt and declining incomes have done nothing to help food security,' says the study.

The government of the *Philippines* has faithfully implemented its commitments under the Uruguay Round. It has liberalized trade and allowed the import of more sugar, an important sector. But when imports from an efficient, low-cost source suddenly started coming into a country that is an inefficient producer, it was small farmers and sugar workers of the Philippines who paid the price – over 400,000 people. Because they are among the poorest sections of the country's population, their food security is at stake. The experience of the Philippines shows the limitations of the neat little world of economic theory, in which trade liberalization appears to make sense by contributing to the more efficient allocation of resources, ensuring that the cheapest producer wins. Such a theory can only be imposed on the complex world that makes up developing country agriculture at enormous human cost – in practice, at a cost to those whose food security is already at risk.

Agribusiness transnational corporations 'have reaped the gains from trade liberalization', concluded the study, but this been accompanied 'by a growing number of hungry people .... [T]he process of economic and trade liberalization calls for an active international civil society as a counterbalance to the power of transnational corporations.' It recommends that member states of the WTO freeze further negotiations 'for at least two years in order to conduct a comprehensive impact assessment of the Agreement on Agriculture'.

India

Free trade 'threatens the very foundations of India's hard-won food security', believes Devinder Sharma, an Indian policy analyst. Since independence in 1946, India – which has some 550 million farmers, 70 per cent of them small and marginal farmers – has focused on ensuring food security and self-sufficiency in agriculture.[4]

But since trade liberalization began in India in 1991 the growth rate of foodgrains has come down:

> it is less than the population growth rate and this is going to be a sad state of affairs for a country like India with one billion people. The focus has also shifted to corporate agriculture. Whereas for small farmers the subsidies have been withdrawn, there is a lot of support now for agribusiness industry and for crops which can be exported. The result is that the good area under staple foods is now shifting to export crops, so we'll have to import staple food.

In 1998, the government removed its barriers to soya beans and edible oil imports; in one year, these imports increased by 300 per cent, and many people in oil seed production are now going out of business. In addition to farmers, one and a half million small oil extractors have closed down. The livelihoods of at least three million people have been destroyed, leaving them without money to buy food.

The oil seed production areas are in the dryland, harsh environment areas of India; many farmers in these areas, already poor, have been driven to desperation.

> Recently we had a spate of suicides in India; 500 farmers committed suicide; I have a fear that more and more farmers will add to that list

now. When you import cheaper food the impact is going to be on employment in agriculture, so unemployment in agriculture is going to increase stupendously in India.... At a time when starvation drives poverty-stricken villagers to take their own lives, the government, carefully following the prescriptions of the WTO and the Confederation of Indian Industry, is working to turn Indian agriculture into a food factory and thereby uproot millions of subsistence farmers.

The dairy sector is among the sectors likely to be affected. Although India is the world's biggest milk producer, the removal of quantitative restrictions on skimmed milk powder means that the EU, the US, Australia and New Zealand are preparing to export low-cost milk to the Indian market, again threatening the livelihoods of millions of small milk producers.

But changes in the deployment of land under food crops give rise to even greater concern. Since 1991 a significant shift has occurred in India's cropping patterns. Land under wheat and rice has increased, while land under some pulses and coarse cereals, the staple foods of the poor and landless, has declined. Land-use and cropping patterns are shifting from low-value foods to exportables, including flowers:

There is tremendous government support for flower cultivation, basically for cut flower exports to Europe. In this kind of situation, it's not the farmers who do flower cultivation, it's business – they look at the dollars they are going to get from the export of flowers. We are spending 136 dollars per hectare on cultivating flowers, and what we earn is just 30 dollars. So we are spending a lot of money to earn a little amount. We can only buy a quarter of the food that we stopped producing.

For the trade in shrimps (see last chapter) the impact on food security is even more serious. 'For every dollar that the shrimp trade earns, more than ten dollars of local food security have been destroyed,' estimates Vandana Shiva. Land in India is also being used for cat and dog food. A French company has been given permission to set up a pet food plant, producing food for cats and dogs in Western countries – 'converting our staple foods into foods for cats and dogs. This is the tragedy.'

According to an OECD report, India stands to gain from full liberalization of trade in foodstuffs, increasing its growth rate by 9.6 per cent a year; while some people will lose their jobs in agriculture, Indian people will be better off. But this is dismissed by Sharma:

I'm always amazed by these kind of analyses. When the WTO initially started after years of GATT, we had a figure of a 400 billion dollar gain for the world as a result of the process; a few years later it came down to 200 billion dollars. And nobody talks about the gain now. In the case of what the OECD is saying, it has a clear interest – India is an important market for their member countries – in saying that India is going to gain. But if you look at the impact on unemployment, on the people who will be thrown out of land, the people will be marginalized further, I don't think that has been worked out.

Farmers speak out in Seattle[5]

Peasant and family farmers from Asia, Africa, Latin America, Europe, the Caribbean and North America spoke in Seattle about their experience of agriculture under the WTO.

Honduran farmer: WTO regulations have extremely destructive effects on small farms in Honduras. Import barriers have come down, permitting the import of cheap food produce from Europe, Canada and the United States. Today, we cannot sell our own farm products on the markets because of these imports. Free trade is for multinationals, it is not for the small peasant farmers.

The small family farmer, growing cereals and vegetables, is going out of business; land ownership is being concentrated in the hands of big multinationals. The credit system has been liberalized, which means that small farmers cannot get any credit. This can be changed only if we have an agricultural policy that gives us access to land, appropriate technology, fair trade, food sovereignty, and the right to produce and consume our own food. This right is undermined by WTO rules, that's the problem. Instead of more food sovereignty, there is less food security.

Mary Malcolm, a small dairy farmer in Jamaica with 14 cows, describes the impact of trade liberalization on her and her family as

> devastating: it is unbelievable, because this is my sole income, producing milk for my husband and myself. I have six children and it is virtually impossible sometimes to survive. The liberalization has given the opportunity to the processors. European Union export subsidies on milk are seriously undermining us, putting us out of the market; milk powder comes in at a cheaper rate than it used to. We cannot compete with this. What we are trying [is] to get our own plant together so that we can get the milk out to the consumers. Over the past two years I have thrown away about 200,000 litres. Sometimes you dump virtually all the milk for a fortnight. Another time you'll get everything sold, which is thank you Jesus.

(EU milk powder imports into Jamaica totalled US$13 million in 1998, and came chiefly from Britain, Germany and the Netherlands, says Action Aid. Milk producers in the EU receive a subsidy of 900 Euro for each tonne of milk powder exported; the world market price is around 1160 Euro a tonne. The EU is giving over 1.7 billion Euro in export subsidies on dairy produce each year; unless these subsidies are stopped, the future of dairy farming in countries like Jamaica is bleak.)

Emma Candawa, representative of the Union of Smallholder Farmers of Malawi, which has 50,000 members:

> our farmers were never told what WTO is, and don't see any benefit from it. On the contrary. Export subsidies are subsidizing farmers in Europe who are exporting their foodstuffs to Mexico. The food from Europe is very cheap and puts us in a very bad situation. Our farmers are worse off, much worse off than before. Either the WTO changes or it should get out of our area.

It is not only in developing countries that trade liberalization is displacing people from their land, and leading to the concentration of land in corporate hands. Asked how the WTO and trade liberalization had affected her, *Denise O'Brien, a diary farmer from Iowa, United States*, who used to work with her husband on their 200-acre farm, said:

I've had to considerably downsize my operations; we could no longer make a living because of the low milk prices that resulted partly because of the WTO, which has influenced the domestic farm policy of the US. It has meant the scrapping of all subsidies to the farmers. Now I'm farming six acres of apples and other fruit, and my husband is working away from the farm.

Many of her neighbours have also gone out of business, she says. The US government policy of trying to get the world to consider food produce as the same as any other industrial produce, is described by O'Brien as

absolutely disastrous. Agriculture is not an industrial produce; the US policy would make our small towns and communities a wasteland. We might continue to produce food but it would be as employees of large corporations. It's time the world woke up to what's happening.

'We are the model of agriculture that all the world is supposed to emulate,' says *Nettie Wiebe, a farmer in Saskatchewan, Canada.*

We are highly industrialized, highly capitalized. We are very export-orientated. I work longer and harder to produce more food to send further away. But while Canada has doubled its exports, we have suffered a severe decline in our income. We are dying, it is killing us. We have given up a lot for this free trade.... Saskatchewan is a windy place. We plant windbreaks to protect our soil. What free trade and the WTO do is to systematically bulldoze away all the windbreaks that have been planted and carefully nurtured to protect food supplies. We have the erosion of people, of culture. The level playing field that people talk about levels all the small players off the field. That's what the bulldozer does. And we don't forget that our land is not an inheritance from our ancestors. It is borrowed from our children.

Mexican farmer: Under the North Atlantic Free Trade Agreement between Canada, Mexico and the United States, Mexico agreed to end subsidies on corn (maize). Cheap US corn flooded into Mexico, people were driven from their rural areas into the cities and the nutritional status of millions has declined.

Zimbabwe

In 1990 Zimbabwe was listed by the World Bank as a 'middle-income' developing country; its people then enjoyed an average annual income of US$640. Also in 1990 the country embarked on an 'Economic Structural Adjustment Programme' (ESAP) – which was soon renamed by the country's poor the 'Extreme Suffering for African People's Programme'. It was an apt description. Eight years after ESAP began, Zimbabwe's average annual income had fallen to US$610. After taking inflation into account, this translates into a huge decline in living standards. In 1998 Zimbabwe was classified by the World Bank as a 'low-income' country. While corruption, cronyism and mismanagement of the economy are partly responsible, it was ESAP that started the rot. And the bald figures hide an even more severe impact on the poor.

ESAP has the standard World Bank–IMF emphasis on trade liberalization, reduction of the budget deficit, higher interest rates, market determination of prices and wages, the ending of food subsidies, and charges for health and education. Farmers have been hit particularly hard. Maize is Zimbabwe's staple food but the price of seed has more than doubled in price. Government support for farmers has been drastically reduced – which in turn has affected food output.

'A rapidly deteriorating economic climate – partly a result of a patchy and ambivalent liberalization process – created further difficulties,' says a study published by the Catholic Institute for International Relations (CIIR).[6] Drought, poor soils, the HIV/AIDS pandemic and the beleaguered land reform programme exacerbated the problems. The main objective of this study was to gain a deeper understanding of how trade liberalization has affected the livelihoods of rural households. It looked particularly at maize marketing. In two districts (Mutasa and Chivi) there was consensus among respondents that basic agricultural inputs such as inorganic fertilizers, hybrid seeds and crop chemicals had become prohibitively expensive for most farmers. This has had a negative impact on their food-security capacity. By contrast, in the period before the introduction of Zimbabwe's ESAP, the government subsidized most important agricultural inputs.

To date ESAP has had a greater impact than the WTO's Agreement on Agriculture measures, says the study. 'Under ESAP, all agricultural parastatals were privatized (including lending institutions), domestic markets were liberalized, domestic prices freed from control as subsidies were removed, and the extension service downsized.'

Zimbabwe's commitments under the Agreement on Agriculture include the removal of import and export subsidies, the removal of subsidies to be replaced by direct income transfers, and reduction of tariffs; in practice however, very little has been implemented under the Agreement.

The Green Box measures of the Agreement on Agriculture (which permit a government to take limited measures to protect its small-holder agriculture, see Chapter 3) 'have not been fully exploited by developing countries in some cases (e.g. Zimbabwe) because structural adjustment commitments left little scope for manoeuvre', says the study.

Since 1997, after significant falls in the value of the Zimbabwe dollar, there has been a return to protectionist policies characterized by a reintroduction of price controls on some basic food items, tariff protection and exchange controls. The reintroduction of price controls on maize, in particular, further undermined producers' income earnings.

Trade liberalization under ESAP covered tariff reform, a supportive exchange rate policy, and improved export provisions. At the time of writing domestic trade in all agricultural products except maize has been liberalized. Until the mid-1980s Zimbabwe exported maize and did not import it. The highest recorded export was in 1984 at more than two million tonnes. Imports of the crop began in earnest in the early 1990s, during the drought period, and have continued to gain momentum since trade liberalization. In 1999 maize imports stood at 390,719 tonnes compared to exports of 299,295, making the country a net importer. The value of food imports generally rose from Z$848.7 million in value in 1995, to Z$1.53 billion in 1997. Domestic producers have therefore faced increasing competition and there have been few effective policy interventions to adapt to the changes.

Focus group discussions were carried out in Mutasa and Chivi districts, net food surplus and deficit areas respectively. In Mutasa, farmers said that the rising cost of hybrid seeds, fertilizer and pesticides has prohibited production. The drought also affected production levels – indirectly, in that loss of cattle limited the use of organic manure, as well as directly. Institutional support from the government extension services has been minimal. Since the privatization of Zimbabwe's Grain Marketing Board, market information has been limited. Farmers who had radios were able to acquire information, while others relied on visitors and bus conductors.

Women, in particular, said that they were the main providers of food security and that the strain was becoming unmanageable. As well as performing all the household chores, they tend their fields and market gardens. With a decrease in remittances from relatives in urban areas, women are now engaging in cross–border trading to pay school fees, buy basic food items and maintain their households. Border trading provides further threats, particularly in relation to the spread of HIV/AIDS, and is often not profitable, according to the women.

Chivi district has less rainfall and poorer soils than Mutasa. Diversification has been more significant in cotton and sunflower. Maize was the third most important cash crop to farmers, but remained the main staple crop. In 1998, only 10 per cent of farmers interviewed in Chivi harvested enough maize for their own consumption. Recommendations from the farmers to government were almost identical to those made by the Mutasa community.

'Domestic trade and agricultural liberalization under the ESAP has had an overall negative impact on the poor and very poor smallholders in Zimbabwe,' the study finds.

> Exogenous shocks have worsened the situation. Areas examined in the study, such as domestic food production (input credit and subsidies, capital expenditure and investment promotion), marketing, and direct income transfers and other safety nets are the primary determinants of the food security of individuals....
>
> Market forces have not successfully addressed the problems surrounding domestic food production. The experiences of the two communities in this survey provide a strong case for entrenching food security as a basic human right, and as a principle for governments and

international organizations including the WTO. Increased investment in research and development, a sound policy of direct income transfers to farmers and an equitable distribution of land to poor farmers through land reforms, should be considered by government. The outcome of the next round of Agreement on Agriculture talks at the WTO will be of vital importance to the food security of the poor in developing countries. Policy changes are likely to affect domestic and international agricultural production, and producer and consumer prices of food and goods. At the same time, protectionist policies pursued by developing countries to cushion the poor against adverse economic shocks could be made more or less feasible.

It is important, the study concludes, that 'international trade and economic policies and their impact on poverty are effectively assessed on a case by case basis before more wide-ranging ones are implemented'.

Milk in Uruguay

Until recently small producers in the west and south of Uruguay provided milk for the domestic and export market through the National Cooperative of Milk Producers (Conaprole); 80 per cent of the cooperative's 6,500 milk producers were small, family-run farms.

The milk market in the Mercosur regional trade grouping (Uruguay, Brazil, Argentina and Paraguay) is huge – 22,000 million litres per year. This has proved very attractive for incoming food TNCs. Uruguay has also been seen by these companies as a good base for regional production and trade, because of benevolent fiscal policies for foreign investors, loans from the national bank to transnational companies, and the increasing deregulation of labour. The Italian multinational Parmalat arrived in 1992. Parmalat and Nestlé compete for Mercosur's market.

The global milk market has been seriously affected by a number of problems including high European subsidies for powdered milk exports to Brazil (a country that absorbs a high proportion of Conaprole's exports). This generated financial problems for the cooperative. Several companies, including Exxel, Unilever, Danone, Bongrain and Leche Pascual, made advances towards Conaprole.

'Externalization policies aimed at subordinating the company to foreign interests are causing the bankruptcy of small milk producers,' said Luis Goichea, Secretary-General of the Association of Workers and Employees of Conaprole; 'we know about the lack of ethics of transnational food companies. They are not concerned with production for food and the healthy sustenance of local people, only making more and more profits with less and less effort.'

Vegetables and fruit have also been affected.

Cheap imports of products such as Chinese garlic, processed tomatoes and onions from Spain, Asian pears, Greek processed peaches and Dutch potatoes; and, from the Mercosur region ... lettuce, red peppers, sweet maize, lentils, apples, grapes, carrots and many other things, mean we cannot compete. When we take our products to the local market, prices have been pressed down ten times by these imported products.[7]

Roses in India

Flowers are taking over the fields of India. Aided and abetted by the government, the area under floriculture multiplies every year. Companies from the Netherlands supply much of the planting material.

Karnataka state was the first to promote floriculture. Its new agricultural policy, initiated in 1995, sowed the seeds of corporate farming which is shifting the focus from cereals to flowers. West Bengal, Tamil Nadu, Andhra Pradesh, Maharashtra and most recently Haryana have become addicted to the heady aroma of flower power. Many of the flowers are exported to Europe.

Hidden below the money which is going into floriculture is a recipe for food insecurity and impending ecological disaster. Turning fertile land from the production of staple goods to the commercial cultivation of flowers will only exacerbate the crisis that threatens the sustainability of India's farming system.

Agricultural experts assert that rose cultivation is far more profitable than farming. In fact, the net foreign exchange earnings from one hectare under rose cultivation is sufficient to import only 1,256 tonnes of food crops. But an additional 4,274 tonnes of food crops and almost 200,000 labour days could be generated if the resources and capital employed in one hectare of rose cultivation were to be used instead for food crops. This clearly establishes the economic viability and social necessity of food crops over flower cultivation.

Also, with a density planting of 60,000 flower plants per hectare, and the need to maintain international quality standards, the use of agrochemicals is very high. On average, two pesticide sprayings a week are necessary to control pests and diseases. Yet since India's national seed policy was relaxed in 1988 to encourage the flower industry, close to 40 new pests and diseases have entered the country.

Floriculture demands water in abundant quantities; the use of groundwater at 212 inches per hectare is four times more than the amount needed for food crops. A trail of negative impacts is being left on soil structure, draining fertility and contaminating the underground drinking water supply. Ultimately the land under intensive flower cultivation is rendered unproductive and barren.[8]

Concern at the World Bank

Probably the most devastating indictment of the damaging effects of trade liberalization on the poor has come in a World Bank paper. This concludes that 'greater openness to trade' has had a negative impact on the income growth of the poorest 40 per cent of people in developing countries. The remaining 60 per cent have benefited, claims the paper. 'Poor farmers, who have never heard of the World Trade Organization, are affected by changes in the prices of their inputs and products,' writes one of the authors.[9]

Coming as it does from the World Bank, this paper is a startling commentary on the bank's policies and on the focus that it claims to be putting on poverty eradication. As the population of developing countries is over five billion people, the 'poorest 40 per cent' amount to over two billion people. This would certainly include the 800 million who lack food security. The World Bank has urged on the pace of trade liberalization, yet admits in one of its papers that the policy has failed the poor and is likely to increase poverty.

Conclusion

The evidence is clear. The above case studies show what is happening on the ground; they are a snapshot of what trade liberalization is doing to food security. The theory that free trade works for the poor has been disapproved by practical realities. Western government ministers claim that trade liberalization works for the poor.[10] Their claim is discredited by the evidence.

Unless an attempt is made to understand the effects of trade liberalization on developing countries, especially as it applies to the food security of rural people, developed countries will continue to push for reduced spending in agriculture, appropriate policies will not be enacted and the rural poor will remain marginalized.

These studies show the immediate, short-term effects of liberalization. But what has happened in the short term is beginning to look ominously as though it will be the pattern for the longer term. Under the present international trading system the economic growth that economists tell us will ride to the rescue of the poor looks increasingly like the Emperor with no clothes.

CHAPTER 6

CORPORATE-MANAGED TRADE: PATENTS

'The world doesn't have free trade,
it has corporate-managed trade' –
Ralph Nader

Transnational corporations – enterprises with economic activities in more than one country – live by trade. The largest 500 TNCs account for about 80 per cent of foreign investment, 70 per cent of world trade and 30 per cent of world output. About a third of international trade is conducted by TNCs within their own organizations – a subsidiary in one country selling to and/or buying from a subsidiary in another, or trading with head office. TNCs are particularly active in the processing and marketing of foodstuffs; it is common for a small number to account for over 80 per cent of the trade in an agricultural product.

Six corporations handle about 85 per cent of world trade in grain, eight TNCs account for between 55 to 60 per cent of world coffee sales, seven account for 90 per cent of the tea consumed in Western countries, three account for 83 per cent of world trade in cocoa, three account for 80 per cent of bananas. Food products account for three-quarters of agricultural trade.[1]

TNCs need a regular supply of primary commodities, preferably enough of an over-supply to keep their prices low. By their demand for export crops, the corporations effectively encourage farmers to grow them, often at the expense of food crops. Because of the need to earn more hard currency to repay foreign debt, developing countries have been encouraged by the World Bank and other donors to give their farmers incentives to grow and to trade agricultural commodities. But this has resulted in the 'over-supply' of many commodities, causing lower world prices, meagre returns for developing countries and prices to farmers below the cost of production – leading to hardship and worsening poverty.

Corporate power

TNCs require land that is in the hands of small-scale food-crop farmers and have the power to get it. The transfer of land from food crops to export crops is increasing rapidly; an extra million hectares a year is going under plantation crops for export markets. Such rapid conversion of land from smallholder agriculture to estates producing for export threatens rural economies, resource-poor farming communities and indigenous peoples. It is likely to increase the migration of people to urban areas.

Size and money give the corporations huge power in developing countries. Cargill, for example, a private US company based in Minneapolis, describes itself as 'an international marketer, processor and distributor of agricultural, food, financial and industrial products with some 79,000 employees in more than 1,000 locations in 72 countries and with business activities in 100 more'. It is the world's largest oil seed trader, the second largest phosphate fertilizer producer, and a major trader in grain, coffee, cocoa, sugar, seeds, malt and poultry. The extent of Cargill's trade in coffee – the largest agricultural earner for developing countries – is seen in comparison to Africa. The company has a greater sales turnover in coffee than the GDP of any of the African countries in which it purchases coffee.

In 1999 Cargill had a turnover of just under US$46 billion – roughly equivalent to the GDPs of the 15 poorest sub-Saharan African countries put together – making it one of the world's 12 largest companies.[2] Descendants of Cargill's founder own 85 per cent of the company.

Cargill's activities very directly affect food security. 'Cargill's corporate goal is to double every five to seven years, but the achievement of this goal requires the occupation of more and more territory, and the expulsion of whole societies from their settlements and their commons.'[3] This shows very clearly how TNC expansion comes at the expense of smallholders.

Cargill has 'structural control of the food system, in terms of integration up and down the food chain'.[4] It has tried to convince developing countries that self-sufficiency in food output is not a practical answer to their problems. 'Expanded trade is necessary to smooth out regional supply swings and harness the productivity of low-cost producers worldwide,' it claims.[5] Self-sufficiency would wrest control of the food chain away from Cargill.

In Southern Africa, Cargill has its own regional trading teams, based in Zimbabwe, who produce trading intelligence and food early warning system reports. The company is probably better informed than the regions's governments about what is going on. It has recently developed ports and water routes around the world to carry forward a policy of seeking access to every major growing region of the world in order to be able to source or originate products wherever they can be obtained most cheaply at any given time.

The 1993 GATT Uruguay Round Agreement strengthened TNCs considerably because it means that governments are less able to regulate and control them. The corporations had a considerable influence over the rules embodied in the agreement. During the talks, 'representatives from TNCs staffed all of the 15 advisory groups set up by the Reagan administration to draw up the US position'.[6]

Under the autocratic secret procedures of the World Trade Organization, TNCs want international patent monopolies, not just on medicines, on seeds, on flora and fauna. The rules are to subjugate the health and safety standards of the member countries to the imperatives of the international trade.[7]

Thus TNCs are using the WTO to try 'to bring into being a global, deregulated market, which they control and in which no robust law intended to protect the environment or human rights will be allowed to survive'.[8]

The development of international markets for agricultural products is leading to monocropping (single crops usually grown on large plots) and creating genetic uniformity. History has shown that large areas planted to single crops are highly vulnerable to new strains of pathogens or insect pests. The widespread use of homogeneous transgenic varieties will unavoidably lead to 'genetic erosion' as the local varieties used by thousands of farmers in the developing world are replaced by the new seeds.

TNCs favour monocropping and, wherever possible, will require farmers to buy their brand of inputs and forbid them from keeping or selling seed. By controlling germplasm from seed to sale, and by forcing farmers to pay inflated prices for seed–chemical packages, TNCs strive to extract maximum profit from their investments.[9] In developing countries there is a particular fear of monopolistic control over food security systems. The system of patents and the corporate role in genetically modified foods pose a potentially huge threat to food security.

Patents and intellectual property rights

Patents are the lifeblood of TNCs. The large corporations especially have the money to research and develop products that are patentable, together with the legal means to protect them; they also have WTO rules on their side. 'Global trade rules on patents permit huge companies to gain control of southern crops at the expense of hungry people.'[10] Yet patents were developed by industrial societies in order to reward inventors of machinery. Around 97 per cent of all the world's patents are held by companies in Western countries. The corporations have not been slow to spread their patenting into the developing world; some 80 per cent of patents for technology and products in developing countries are now held by TNCs.

In the 1990s, TNCs began to take out patents on plant species, most of which are found in Africa, Asia and Latin America. They argue that they can only afford to invest large sums of money in breeding activities if their investment is protected. Among non-governmental organizations, however, there is broad agreement that patents are not appropriate for life forms such as plants, which have been developed over centuries.

Through patenting, the North is seeking to exploit what is essentially a Southern resource. Biodiversity is a key resource, both for people in developing countries and for the billion-dollar biotechnology industry. Herein lie the seeds of the conflict. The key question is whether this resource is harnessed for food security, for the survival of millions, or is patented for the benefit of a small number of TNCs and their shareholders.

A weakness of the Uruguay Round agreement is that it does not distinguish between formal industrial innovation and exploitation of plant material. Patents on plants mean that Third World farmers have to pay the corporations high prices for 'improved' varieties. Such patents are becoming attractive to TNCs because plant resources are becoming more valuable. Their potential value and the possibilities that are opened up by biotechnology, patents, and plant breeders' rights have caused the corporations to get involved in a big way. The 1970s witnessed a huge entry of multinational chemical corporations into the crop breeding sector, with hundreds of small family seed companies taken over.

The idea of a company 'owning' a plant variety is new in agriculture. Traditionally, even newly developed varieties of crops such as rice have always been made freely available to all farmers. Concepts such as intellectual property rights are in danger of changing long-cherished traditions that have seen varieties shared freely not only among poor farmers but also among nations. The spread of patented crop varieties is likely to work against the sharing of varieties, and against food security.

Laws governing the inventions that can be patented vary from country to country. The United States was the first country to grant patents on plant varieties and is practically alone in allowing patents on life forms. Other countries have judged patent systems to be unsuitable for living organisms. India, for example, which has around 15,000 plant varieties unique to the country, does not allow patents to be taken out on them. The Indian Patents Act of 1970 makes it clear that inventions relating to agricultural and horticultural processes are not patentable on the grounds that socially valuable products ought not to be privatized or priced out of the reach of the general public.

The Uruguay Round agreement on TRIPs effectively globalizes the patent system. 'Patents on rice, sorghum, cassava, maize, millet, potato, soybean and wheat are falling into company hands ... this raises questions for food security.'[11]

Trade-Related Intellectual Property Rights

The Uruguay Round agreement on TRIPs provides comprehensive rules and standards for intellectual property rights that are related to international trade. It came into force in January 1995 and grants corporations the right to protect their 'intellectual property' in all member countries of the WTO. The agreement protects the interests of the TNCs and is a curious departure from the free trade principles of the WTO (see below).

The TRIPs accord is the most comprehensive international agreement on intellectual property rights and supplements World Intellectual Property Organization conventions with substantive obligations under WTO rules. Article 27.3b of the agreement allows countries to exclude plants and animals from patentability, but still requires some form of intellectual property protection for new plant varieties.

Because of the agreement's rules on the patenting of life forms, especially seeds, TRIPs has a direct bearing on food security. It means that if a process to produce a plant is patented, 'the owner of the patent has exclusive rights over the plants obtained using the process. Farmers are not allowed to use any seeds coming from such a plant.'[12] Again the concern is that through the patenting of seeds TNCs will gain control over the food crops of the poor.

The TRIPs agreement was the brainchild of an industry coalition made up of people from the United States, the European Union and Japan. The first initiative was taken by the Intellectual Property Committee, which brings together 13 major US corporations including Bristol Myers Squibb, Du Pont, Monsanto and General Motors.

The Committee was created during the Uruguay Round negotiations with the explicit goal of putting TRIPs firmly on the agenda.

According to a former Monsanto employee, one of the Intellectual Property Committee's first tasks was 'missionary work' in Europe and Japan in order to gather the support of corporate heavyweights for the TRIPs campaign. Edmund T. Pratt, a former Pfizer chief who attended numerous GATT negotiations in the capacity of official adviser to the US Trade Representative, confirmed that 'our combined strength enabled us to establish a global private sector government network which laid the groundwork for what became TRIPs'. In 1988, following a lobby campaign both in Geneva and at the national level, an industry paper on the 'Basic Framework for GATT Provisions on Intellectual Property' made it into the Uruguay Round negotiations. Not surprisingly, the position put forth by the influential US delegation was strikingly similar to the industry proposal.[13]

The TRIPs agreement is hugely controversial

> because it recognizes patents on plants that have been developed though biotechnology using plant varieties that themselves are the [result of] years of cross-breeding by farmers. This implies that TRIPs does not recognize communities' rights over their resources.[14]

But this 'creates potential for disastrous conflicts between technologically advanced and less technologically advanced countries'.[15]

Intellectual property rights establish private, exclusive, monopolistic control over plant genetic resources, resulting in farmer dislocation and the loss of food security. Such 'rights' can deprive farmers of *their* rights – the right to develop and exchange their own seed, and, ultimately, the right of survival.

In India the controversy over TRIPs has generated considerable feeling. Farmers in Karnataka state burnt down an administrative building belonging to Cargill because they were fearful that the TRIPs provision could make it illegal for them to replant seeds that their ancestors have used for centuries without paying royalties to patent holders. 'The installation of a patents regime in genes, plants and farm inputs, when none exists, is to gain control of a nation covertly,' says M.D. Nanjundaswamy, president of the Karnataka Farmers' Association.[16]

While awareness of the issues is generally high among farmers in countries such as India, it tends to be lower among governments of developing countries. During the TRIPs negotiations, concern about the ethical implications of the private ownership of life prompted some Southern countries to oppose the patenting of life forms. But most

> signed up to TRIPs as part of a package deal, a trade off for elements in other WTO agreements, rather than because they wanted it.... [M]any signed it without any clear analysis of its implications – in part due to the difficulties facing poor countries in taking part in such technically complex, multi-faceted negotiations.[17]

The TRIPs agreement committed WTO member countries to introducing patent laws on life forms by January 2000 (the least-developed countries were allowed up to 2005). But this process involved substantial legislative changes and the deadline was widely ignored. In July 1999 African countries urged that discussions over TRIPs should be staggered and sequenced in a manner that enables developing countries with meagre resources to participate effectively. At a meeting of the Group of 15 developing countries in August 1999 Venezuela proposed that developing countries be allowed a five-year extension (from 2000) to implement the TRIPs agreement. Such was the disarray at the Seattle ministerial meeting that no decisions were taken.

A further problem with the TRIPs agreement is that it is in contra-vention of the UN Convention on Biological Diversity (CBD) which came into force in 1993. This convention 'seeks to promote the estab-lishment of sovereign, community and indigenous rights to the bio-logical resources of the South'. The CBD 'is rooted in the principle that benefits from using genetic resources should be shared. However TRIPs promotes the privatization of genetic resources, not benefit sharing.'[18]

Two legally binding agreements, TRIPs and the CBD, are there-fore in direct conflict with each other. Many in the South are coming to see the CBD as a means of counter-balancing the rights granted in TRIPs. But WTO agreements, such as TRIPs, are held by Western countries to be virtually unchallengeable. For the South, however, it is the CBD and not TRIPs that should be the guiding policy. Another international accord, the voluntary International Undertaking on Plant Genetic Resources, adopted in 1983, seeks to protect countries and farmers from the exploitation of their genetic resources. The Undertaking is at present voluntary but is being revised. Developing countries want it to be made legally binding.

Farmer knowledge of genetic resources has contributed enormously to the people and companies of the North, but without 'royalties' being paid to farmers in South for the use of this 'intellectual property'. Whereas there was no question of farmers taking out patents on their improvements to seeds, TNCs are trying to patent new seed varieties that they claim to have 'invented' – but which farmers have helped to develop down the centuries.

Indigenous peoples also feel cheated. At the Seattle ministerial meeting, representatives of indigenous peoples expressed strong concern about intellectual property rights. 'The theft and patenting of our biogenetic resources is facilitated by the TRIPs agreement,' said a declaration by indigenous peoples.

> Some plants which indigenous peoples have discovered, cultivated, and used for food, medicine, and for sacred rituals are already patented in the United States, Japan, and Europe. A few examples of these are *ayahuasca*, *quinoa*, and *sangre de drago* in forests of South America; *kava* in the Pacific; turmeric and bitter melon in Asia. Our access and control over our biological diversity and control over our traditional knowledge and intellectual heritage are threatened by the TRIPs Agreement. Article 27.3b of [this] agreement allows the patenting of life forms and makes an artificial distinction between plants, animals, and micro-organisms. As far as we are concerned all these are life forms and life-creating processes which are sacred and which should not become the subject of private property ownership.[19]

TNCs are making handsome profits out of the knowledge of Third World farmers, indigenous peoples and their biodiversity. The Canada-based Rural Advancement Foundation International (RAFI) has compiled a list of well over a hundred cases in which genetic resources and/or local knowledge in the South have made – or are making – a contribution to agriculture, food processing or pharmaceutical development in the North. They include Bayer's synthetic aspirin, the world's most widely used drug, which is derived from a traditional Arab medicinal plant.

Wheat material from the Mexico-based International Maize and Wheat Improvement Centre is estimated to contribute US$3.1 billion annually to the total farmgate value of the US wheat crop. *Pau D'Arc*, a medicinal plant from Latin America used to combat malaria and cancers, has a market value in the North of US$200 million a year. According to a RAFI report prepared for the UNDP, contributions of plant genetic resources and knowledge from farmers in the South are worth US$4.5 billion a year to the North.[20]

Biopiracy

Companies – sometimes through academic research departments, whom they sponsor – are taking plant species from developing countries without permission and without offering any compensation. In 1999 RAFI documented 147 suspected cases of institutional 'biopiracy'. Examples from Gabon, Thailand, Ecuador and Peru illustrate biopiracy activities on a grand scale, it says. In one of these cases, the University of Wisconsin has received two US patents for a berry from a plant that grows in Gabon called *Pentadiplandra brazzeana*. The berries were collected by a University of Wisconsin researcher working in Gabon who found that a sweet protein could be derived from the berries.[21] The University of Wisconsin now has its patents for the protein which it calls 'brazzein' and which, it claims, is 2,000 times sweeter than sugar. The university now intends to license its exclusive rights to brazzein to corporations. 'Wisconsin believes it can make inroads into the US$100 billion a year worldwide market for sweeteners,' says RAFI. Yet Gabon is unlikely to receive anything for its contribution to the development of the new sweetener.

An Action Aid report says that 62 patents 'show some evidence of biopiracy ... such patents are enabling companies in rich nations to exploit crops at the expense of poor farmers and their families'.[22] There is also a danger that patents will intensify the problems of substitution, it warns, allowing TNCs to speed up the development of substitutes for crops that are grown in developing countries, displacing traditional producers.

Stealing the 'crown jewel'

Basmati, the 'crown jewel' of South Asian rice, is prized for its fragrant aroma, its long, slender grain and distinctive taste; it commands a premium price in both domestic and international markets. A million hectares in India and three-quarters of a million in Pakistan are planted out to basmati varieties. Cultivated by hundreds of thousands of small farmers, the rice has been grown for centuries in the two countries, with farmers selecting and maintaining the varieties. In India alone, basmati exports were valued at US$425 million in 1998/9.

In September 1997 the Texas-based RiceTec Inc., a small company with 120 employees, won a controversial US patent on basmati rice. 'RiceTec's basmati patent has become widely known as a classic case of biopiracy,' says RAFI, for 'not only does the patent usurp the basmati name, it also capitalises on the genius of South Asian farmers. The patent applies to breeding crosses involving 22 farmer-bred basmati varieties from Pakistan and India.' The sweeping scope of the patent extends to such varieties grown anywhere in the western hemisphere (although the patent is valid only in the US).

In 1998, the Indian government appointed an expert technical committee to review the basmati patent. The committee compiled and reviewed over 1,500 pages of background information that will form the basis for challenging the RiceTec patent, and specifically for refuting the company's claims of novelty. According to the patent, RiceTec's invention includes the discovery that the likely texture of cooked rice can be predicted by measuring a grain's 'starch index'. According to K. R. Bhattacharya, former head of the Department of Grain Science of the Central Food Technological Research Institute in Mysore, India, 'the so-called relation of starch index to rice cooking behaviour is fallacious, artificial, false and fake; and that it is strongly suggestive of being deliberately got up to manufacture a patentable claim'.[23] Critics of the basmati patent have argued that RiceTec's use of the name 'basmati' is a misrepresentation because only rice grown in northern India and Pakistan can be so termed. The TRIPs agreement provides for protection where a given quality or reputation of an item is attributable to its geographic origin.

Motivated by the basmati debacle, the Indian government is preparing to introduce the Geographical Indication of Goods' Registration and Protection Act, which seeks to provide protection for goods rendered distinctive by their quality or uniqueness and would establish a national registry of such items. In addition to basmati, the legislation would protect other unique goods of Indian origin such as Darjeeling tea, Alphonso mangoes, Malabar pepper or Alappuzha cardamom.

India, Switzerland, the European Union, the Czech Republic, Morocco and others have strongly advocated strengthening and widening the protection of geographical indications for agricultural products under Article 23 of TRIPs. That article, which currently applies only to wines and spirits, prevents the use of expressions – such as 'kind', 'type' or 'imitation' – which could mislead the public as to the geographic origin of the product.

'Marketing rice varieties developed by crossing semi-dwarf varieties with Basmati rice from India/Pakistan, as American Basmati is unethical. This is designed to kill even the limited opportunities which poor developing countries have for farm exports,' says Dr M. S. Swaminathan, one of the world's leading rice experts.

'The basmati patent is viewed as an unreasonable intellectual property claim on crop varieties or traits of distinct national origin,' says Dr Gordon Conway, president of the US-based Rockefeller Foundation, which has invested over US$100 million over the past 15 years in plant biotechnology research, principally for rice.[24]

In its code of practice for rice, the UK's Grain and Feed Trade Association, one of the world's largest importers of basmati rice, also concludes that basmati rice 'shall only be applied to the long grain rice grown in India or Pakistan'. Similarly, Saudi Arabia allows basmati rice originating only in the Indian sub-continent to be sold as basmati rice.' Saudi Arabia accounted for 68 per cent of India's basmati exports in 1994.

'It is indecent and unacceptable for the genius of millennia to be usurped by a US-based company. RiceTec's patent is predatory on the rights and resources of South Asian farmers, and it should be abandoned,' believes RAFI.

The future

A patenting system that is suitable for intensive, industrialized farming systems is unlikely to be suitable in developing countries where subsistence farming is the chief form of agriculture.

> The global application of the TRIPs Agreement is in danger of imposing on poor societies and communities an alien set of concepts of property .... [T]he impact of intellectual property rights on who is developing what, who will control innovations and in whose interests is vitally important for future food security.[25]

Farmers in developing countries are concerned that if patents on crops were granted, TNCs would jeopardize their independence and push them off their land, and that genetically uniform varieties would spread faster, giving them less choice. Farmers want the right to save, use and exchange the seeds that they have helped to develop over many years. They want the assurance that their farming systems will not be undermined by patents, and that if a company is claiming breeders' rights on a variety then they, the farmers, have the right to plant that variety without asking permission or paying royalties.

The TRIPs agreement does allow countries to set up their own *sui generis* systems of intellectual property rights to patents.

> The US and EU say that any *sui generis* legislation should be based on the Union for the Protection of New Varieties of Plants (UPOV). But UPOV gives breeders exclusive ownership over the commercial use of plant varieties and accepts patents on transgenic varieties to which the developing world objects.[26]

'TRIPs is a cunning trap; it invites countries to devise *sui generis* legislation in a seemingly open manner, but it is clear that any *sui generis* law ... has to be an intellectual property system.'[27] 'Developing countries need to bring in tougher national legislation to prevent unauthorized collection of germplasm, especially by the multinationals,' believes Devinder Sharma.[28] Many countries have already imposed such bans, he says, including Ethiopia, Iran, Iraq and China.

Action Aid has urged the WTO to support an amendment to Article 27.3b of the TRIPs agreement that would enable member countries to exclude all genetic resources for food and agriculture from the agreement. There have also been calls for TRIPs to be taken out of the WTO. 'The TRIPs agreement has no business to be at the WTO; it should be sent to the World Intellectual Property Organization, which has the mandate,' believes Pradeep Mehta, Secretary-General of the Jaipur-based Centre for International Trade, Economics and Environment.[29]

A further potential threat to food security, warns Action Aid, is the race in which the corporations are involved to map the genes of staple food crops, 'often at huge expense, in order to gain patents'.[30] The whole business of patenting is stacked in favour of TNCs and against the interests of small farmers. It further strengthens TNC power to manage international trade. If the international community wants to keep its commitment to halving the number of hungry people by 2015, it should change its patent rules to protect resource–poor farmers.

CHAPTER 7

CORPORATE-MANAGED TRADE: GENETICALLY MODIFIED FOODS

By early 2000 about 100 million acres were under genetically modified crops, chiefly soya and maize, grown on large capital-intensive farms in the US, Canada, Argentina and Mexico (although in China mostly small farmers had a million acres under these crops). More than half the soya beans in the US were grown with the GM seeds of Monsanto (or Pharmacia, as it now wants to be known). Most of the global output of GM crops has so far gone for animal feed; while only a small proportion has been offered for direct human consumption, people are consuming these foods indirectly through animals.

The GM food industry is dominated by five large companies – Monsanto, Astra Zeneca, Du Pont, Novartis and Aventis. In the US, Monsanto controls 88 per cent of the GM seed market. These companies need to trade genetically modified crops across borders to realize their profit potential. The European market holds big attractions, but all companies are eyeing the Third World market. If they can persuade policy makers that GM seeds, crops and foods are essential scientific breakthroughs needed to feed the world and reduce poverty in developing countries, that they are the key to food security, then the business has an assured future. But policy makers in developing countries show few signs of being convinced.

The trade rules embodied in the WTO are relevant to GM crops for a number of reasons – they could limit the rights of countries to restrict production and trade of GM products, to introduce mandatory labelling of foods, or to design their own intellectual property legislation (see Chapter 6). Trade in GM crops expanded rapidly in the late 1990s to around US\$2 billion by 2000. But the refusal of most of the world – from the European Union countries to Thailand – to import these crops and seeds is limiting growth. In late 1996 Monsanto released a genetically engineered soya bean, predicting that genetically altered seed would become a US\$6 billion annual market within five years. This figure seems unlikely to be reached.

Several years after their introduction, there is no evidence that GM crops are capable of yielding more food per hectare of land. A study by the United States Department of Agriculture Economic Research Service shows that in 1998 yields of GM crops were not significantly better than conventional varieties. This was confirmed in another study examining more than 8,000 field trials which found that Roundup Ready soya bean seeds produced fewer bushels of soya beans than similar conventionally bred varieties.[1]

GM crops were certainly not designed by the corporations to benefit small farmers in developing countries. The concern of these farmers is that GM technology will be damaging for their own agriculture and for food security, not least by giving TNCs monopoly control over food supplies. 'Food security means that local communities must have the capacity to access, develop and exchange seeds and produce enough food for households .... [T]he lethal use of genetic engineering technology threatens the food security of this and future generations,' says Wangari Maathai, of Kenya's Greenbelt Movement.[2]

Farmers in India have been especially vociferous, seeing GM technology as a threat to their livelihoods, giving corporations an unacceptable degree of control over them. It would mean they would have to buy GM seeds each year from the company. Companies that control seed supplies, control food supplies. 'The GM issue is perhaps the greatest threat to food security because it transfers the ownership of seed and the food production process to the monopoly control of the TNCs.'[3] TNCs are 'actively developing opportunities to sell their (GM) technology in the South .... [They] have established joint programmes with several private companies and public research organizations in the South.'[4]

Africans, too, are opposing the technology. At a meeting in June 1998 of the UN Food and Agriculture Organization's Commission on Genetic Resources, 24 delegates of African governments issued a statement saying that an advertising campaign by Monsanto 'gives a totally distorted and misleading picture of the potential of genetic engineering to feed developing countries'. It said that they 'strongly object that the image of the poor and hungry from our countries is being used by giant multinational corporations to push a technology that is neither safe, environmentally friendly nor economically beneficial to us'.

The delegates feared that gene technologies 'will destroy the diversity, local knowledge and sustainable agricultural systems that our farmers have developed for millennia, and that it will thus undermine our capacity to feed ourselves'. Western science can contribute to improving agricultural production in Africa, they said, 'but it should be done on the basis of understanding and respect for what is already there'.[5] 'Africa should not be used as testing ground for technologies and products which have been developed elsewhere,' said the Zimbabwe delegate, Shadrack Mlambo, and 'we reserve our sovereign right to test these technologies ourselves, examine their effectiveness and compatibility to the region'.[6]

The spark which lit the GM foods debate was the development in early 1998 by a US-based company, Delta and Pine Land, of seeds which only germinate for one season. Officially known as 'Technology Protection System' it was dubbed 'Terminator technology' as it stops reproduction of viable seed entirely; the second generation is sterile. It would therefore 'terminate' the ancient farmer practice of saving seed from one season for use in the next. While only cotton and tobacco seeds were known to have responded to the technology, Delta and Pine Land apparently intended to apply it to foods such as wheat and rice; other crops could follow. Later in 1998, Monsanto agreed to acquire the company. Patents for the technology were soon applied for in over 80 countries.

Monsanto took the view that the system would benefit the world agricultural community because it means that farmers in all areas of the world have an opportunity to share in the advantage of improved seed. Other companies, too, were developing Terminator technologies. By early 1999 genetic seed sterilization had emerged as a major corporate ambition. 'Virtually all of the world's largest seed and agrochemical corporations were then working on the goal of genetic seed sterilization,' says RAFI.[7]

Most small-scale Third World farmers could not afford to buy new seed each year; borrowing money for seed would be risky and is in any case difficult, owing to the unwillingness of the banking sector in most developing countries to lend to farmers who cannot offer any collateral. Rural moneylenders charge farmers such exorbitant rates as to make borrowing uneconomic. Even if credit was available to farmers, however, many farmers take the view that food crop seed is too important to be in the hands of outside companies and should remain under local control and development.

Scientists and crop breeders as well as farmers criticized the technology on the grounds that Terminator would affect the breeding of new crops. The Consultative Group on International Agricultural Research (CGIAR) – a network of 16 international research stations – announced a ban on the technology because of the way that it would block crop breeding.

In October 1999, after 18 months of controversy and intense opposition around the world, the chief executive of Monsanto, Robert Shapiro, said that the company would heed public concern about sterile seed technologies and not commercialize the technology.[8] 'The public unanimously rejected Terminator because it's bad for farmers, food security and the environment,' says Pat Mooney of RAFI.[9]

Terminator technology is a 'genetic use restriction technology' (GURT). And while Monsanto said it would abandon the Terminator, it was still developing another type of genetic use restriction technology, called a trait GURT. 'Monsanto holds patents on technological approaches to gene protection that do not render seeds sterile,' says Shapiro, in an apparent reference to this type of restriction technology.[10]

In trait GURTs, an inhibiting function operates at the gene level. A plant may be able to produce viable seed but certain traits (for example, drought or disease resistance) will not be present a second time unless external chemicals are applied. The UK-based company Astra Zeneca has developed a technology, (dubbed the 'Verminator', because the gene is taken from mice), that would not allow genetically engineered seed to germinate unless it was triggered by the company's chemicals. This trait GURT addicts plants to chemicals rather than killing seed. Swiss-based Novartis has developed a technique to use a trait GURT to disable a plant's natural disease resistance, making it more likely to require chemicals. The companies have naturally taken out patents on their technologies. The number of patents on GURTs has dramatically expanded, according to RAFI. 'The need for companies to protect and gain a return on their investments in agricultural innovation is real,' says Robert Shapiro.[11]

'It's all part of efforts by the companies to gain control over seed supplies,' believes Pete Riley of Friends of the Earth, UK:

> the traits the companies plan to build into the seeds are designed to help them sell more pesticides and so on, rather than to benefit the farmer. It's healthy for global seed supplies to be as diverse as possible, spread over many different hands rather than under the control of a few powerful companies.[12]

'We can't trust where the technology and companies may be taking us,' is the verdict of Pat Mooney. 'The technology for seed sterilization and trait control are on the same trajectory. At some point, either through a corporate takeover or a change in management, trait control could easily be transformed back into genetic seed sterilization.'[13] Three months after Shapiro's announcement, there was another by Harry Collins of Delta and Pine Land: 'We've continued right on with work on the Technology Protection System [Terminator]. We never really slowed down. We're on target, moving ahead to commercialize it. We never really backed off.'[14] It seemed that little had changed.

A number of people in senior Western government positions have questioned the benefits of GM technology, including Dan Glickman, US Agriculture Secretary. Glickman has highlighted 'the danger of small farmers becoming dependent on privately owned technologies, including GM, noting that profit-driven choices in technology development are at best irrelevant to poor farmers and, at worst, reduces them to serfs on the land'.[15]

Could GM crops play a role in food security? At best their contribution seems likely to be limited and costly. 'The new technologies are expensive to develop, estimated at US$1 million per gene, and companies are expecting to recoup costs as well as make large profits on sales.'[16] Advocates appear to be concentrating on specific benefits, rather than yields. 'Some 3 million children go blind each year because of Vitamin A deficiency. The best hope of tackling this is through Vitamin A enriched plant materials, and genetic modification provides probably the best hope. We need to set benefits like this against risks.'[17]

Research is also being done into varieties of crops with genes which have resistance to salinity, drought and diseases. Scientists at the Madras-based M. S. Swaminathan Research Foundation, for example, are trying to transfer coastal salinity tolerance to rice. These desirable traits are difficult to engineer; the innovations could take at least 10 years before they reach the farmer (see box on p. 117). It should also be noted that conventional crop breeding – already the source of a number of wheats with high tolerance to drought – could provide answers to these problems.

In January 2000 researchers claimed to have developed a yellow rice with a high Vitamin A content. But considerable progress has already been made 'towards achieving the UN goal of virtually eliminating Vitamin A deficiency disorders', said the World Health Organization in 1999.[18] The number of young children affected by these disorders has fallen by about two-thirds in the past 20 years. Should this rate continue, the disorders will have been eliminated within ten years – probably before the GM crop becomes available.

Ironically, before the 'green revolution', many rice varieties *did* contain Vitamin A. This diversity was largely destroyed because of the application of 'advanced technologies'. Inventing GM crops with Vitamin A would be to invent something which nature had already provided in abundance.

Vitamin A deficiency occurs because of poverty – people are not able to grow or buy a suitable range of foods; their family diet does not include all the necessary food values . The vitamin is found in animal foods such as fish, liver, breastmilk, egg yolk and dairy products, and also in plant food, particularly yellow and red fruits (mangoes, papaws) and red palm oil. Vitamin A deficiency disorders can be overcome by tackling poverty, without taking the risk of GM foods.

Should GM crops with positive attributes be developed, questions would still remain about safety and the impact on the environment. Possibly the most pressing question is: who controls the seeds of the new crops – large transnationals or smallholder farmers? In practice, it will be TNCs, leaving smallholders in a subservient position, and leaving society with little or no democratic control over the supply of these foods.

NGOs and GM foods

NGOs differ on the future of GM crops. Oxfam UK believes that

> leaving aside risk factors, GM crops could be of some benefit to poor farmers in the longer term if applications are directed to their needs and if intellectual property rules do not channel all the gains to companies. These conditions do not apply at present and require government action.

It sees the 'need for public investment and incentives to promote private investment in GM research and innovation benefiting poor farmers and low income consumers'. Oxfam recommends that donor governments and agencies commit resources for investment in research into the potential opportunities presented by applications of GM technology to deliver environmental and health benefits pertaining to smallholder agriculture.[19]

This appears, however, to be a minority view among NGOs on the GM food issue, and draws strong criticism from Vandana Shiva:

Oxfam risks betraying the South, the poor and food security objectives by calling for support for promotion of GM crops in the South instead of calling for support for ecological and sustainable agriculture which is much better suited to the small farmers in adverse agro-ecological zones.... Research from our own programmes in India and studies worldwide are countering the myth that ecological agriculture has low productivity and low returns. Farmers in fact have a tripling of incomes by getting off the chemical treadmill and getting out of the debt trap created by purchase of costly seeds and chemicals. Because GM-free agriculture is good for the poor and good for the environment. We have launched the 'Bija Satyagraha' which includes the creation of GM-free zones in agriculture as part of the National Food Rights Campaign in India, in which more than 2,500 groups participate.[20]

Oxfam's endorsement, it should be noted, contains several cautionary reservations.

Once available and if farmers can afford them [GM crops], the contribution to yield enhancement of such varieties will be between 20–35 per cent; the rest of yield increases must come from agricultural management.... There may be gains to low-income consumers flowing from reduced crop prices, if there are not effective monopolies in the supply chain. There should be an international moratorium on the commercial growing of GM crops to allow further scientific assessment of socioeconomic, health and environmental impacts; public debate on biotechnology; establishment of national regulatory systems, and adoption of legislation creating company liability for adverse effects.[21]

Labelling

GM food manufacturers in the United States are not required to label their products and inform consumers that they are buying food containing GM ingredients. The European Commission approved a regulation in January 2000 that requires food companies to state on the labels of their products if any ingredient contains 1 per cent or more of GM soya or maize. The Commission is likely to extend this to other products. It is also working on plans that would require food companies to put 'GM-free' on their labels.

The question is whether such labelling could be challenged by the US as a restraint of the trade of its GM manufacturers. While the US has not so far resorted to the WTO disputes settlement panel on the issue, it has put pressure on developing countries to toe the US line. In June 1998, for example, Egypt announced its intention to ban the import of GM foods from the United States unless they were properly labelled. The US responded to Egypt's move by threatening to ban all trade between the two countries in soya beans and maize. Egypt reversed its decision.

'WTO rules may permit successful challenges to the labelling of GM foods,' Ralph Nader points out.

> Just as the Clinton administration has argued against labelling of biotech foods in the United States on the grounds that they are equivalent to conventional foods, so it argues that other countries' initiatives to label genetically altered foods is not based on international standards or on sound science, and is therefore WTO-illegal.[22]

Developing countries are generally adopting the 'precautionary principle' over genetically modified organisms (GMOs) – they are not importing GM food products, or at the very least want them labelled as a precaution against possible health and environmental risks. Before the agreement on the BioSafety Protocol (see below) this policy could have been challenged under WTO rules.

NGOs want the precautionary principle to become a central part of international agreements. 'If there is no widely accepted scientific evidence that GMOs are safe, the precautionary principle should prevail – that countries should go slow, pending evidence. Under this principle, the burden of proof lies with the developer,' believes Doreen Stabinsky of the US-based Council for Responsible Genetics.[23]

Protocol

An international BioSafety Protocol to regulate trade in GM organisms was agreed by government ministers at Montreal in January 2000.

The agreement is significant in that it allows countries to follow the precautionary principle on GMOs. It permits countries to ban the import of GM crops if they are concerned over their safety, without having to give scientific proof. The Protocol is not subordinate to other international agreements, says its preamble. Since this would clearly include the World Trade Organization, a government that bans GMOs cannot be challenged under the WTO's disputes settlement procedure.

The Protocol is the first international agreement to recognize that the precautionary principle should prevail, the first to put safety above trade. The WTO's power seems therefore to have been checked by another international agreement. 'For the first time, countries will have the right to decide whether they want to import GM products or not, when there is less than full scientific evidence. It's official that environmental rules aren't subordinate to the trade rules.'[24]

The Cartagena Protocol on BioSafety, as it will be called, took six years to negotiate and will come under the Convention on Biological Diversity (CBD), which was agreed at the 1992 Earth Summit in Brazil. It takes the name Cartagena because negotiations to establish the Protocol started at a conference in Cartagena, Colombia, in February 1999. The breakdown of negotiations in Cartagena was related to a US–EU disagreement over GM crop regulation and labelling, and the relationship of the proposed Protocol to trade agreements.

The European Union and the vast majority of developing countries argued during negotiations that importing countries should have the right to reject GMOs, including food ingredients. They wanted a wide-ranging Protocol that would protect biodiversity from the threat posed by GMOs, partly because the loss of biodiversity puts food security at risk. The Miami Group of agricultural exporting countries – Argentina, Australia, Canada, Chile, Uruguay and the USA – wanted a weak Protocol that was subordinate to WTO rules.

The signing of the Protocol 'is a campaign victory in that it acknowledges that GMOs are not the same as other crops and products and they require that special measures be taken,' said Mariam Mayet of the Malaysia-based Third World Network.[25] Under the Protocol, countries will be to choose whether they wish to import conventionally bred crops or GM crops. It gives developing countries 'the right to say no to GM seeds that could cause massive damage to the livelihoods of small farmers', believes Barry Coates, director of the World Development Movement; 'perhaps even more significantly, it may signal the end of the mad dash for liberalization at all costs. The spectacular derailment of the free trade juggernaut in Seattle has created political space for alternatives.'[26]

The Protocol is, however, a compromise. For the preamble also states that the Protocol 'shall not be interpreted as implying a change in the rights and obligations of a party under existing international agreements'. It seems that the Protocol will have 'equal status with international trade rules and international obligations'.[27] Most developing countries wanted a Protocol that would require exporters to label any commodity that contains GMOs, but the Miami group countries blocked any mandatory labelling requirement on the part of food companies and exporters. Exporters will be required instead to label foods if they 'may' contain GMOs. It will also require countries to notify others if they approve new GM seeds or crops. While the Protocol is therefore not as strong as campaigners had hoped, it is important in that it challenges the principle that free trade rules are always paramount.

A declining market for GM foods throughout the world was a reason why the US and other grain exporters were persuaded that a Protocol was necessary. If the market for these foods is not to disappear altogether, then the US needed to build public trust; some regulation of the trade was its only option. Despite the Protocol, and controls on the trade in GM seeds and crops, TNCs could still try to introduce the technology into developing countries, putting small-scale farmers at risk. 'It's a case of policy versus capacity,' according to Debbie Dying of the Intermediate Technology Development Group in Zimbabwe; 'our Government simply does not have the capacity to monitor this technology on its own and companies are moving too quickly.'[28]

Conclusion

Hunger is not due to a gap between food production and human population density or growth rate. Genetic engineering is not the only or best way to increase agricultural production and meet future food needs. GM crops are not relevant to the main reason why people go hungry, namely, lack the money to buy food or the land on which to grow it. Hunger does not happen because of any absolute shortage of food supplies. Enough food is already grown to provide everyone with an adequate diet. In Africa, as elsewhere, people can go hungry even when food is plentiful in local markets.

'There are still hungry people in Ethiopia, but they are hungry because they have no money, not because there is no food to buy,' says Tewolde Egziabher of the Institute for Sustainable Development in Addis Ababa. Lack of rights and political muscle to influence policy were identified as factors behind Sudan's famine in the 1980s. The availability of GM foods will not overcome such underlying problems. Political and economic rights, stability, access to land and money to buy food are seen as more important. Only if GM technology is democratized and brought under farmer control is it likely to gain wide acceptance.

Food, the Environment and Poverty:

Ten Reasons Why Biotechnology Will Not Deliver

Miguel A. Altieri and Peter Rosset challenge the notion of biotechnology as a magic bullet solution to agriculture's ills.

1   There is no relationship between the prevalence of hunger in a given country and its population. For every densely populated and hungry nation like Bangladesh or Haiti, there is a sparsely populated and hungry nation like Brazil and Indonesia.

2   Most innovations in agricultural biotechnology have been profit-driven rather than need-driven. The real thrust of the genetic engineering industry is not to make Third World agriculture more productive, but rather to generate profits. This is illustrated by reviewing the principle technologies on the market today: herbicide resistant crops such as Monsanto's Roundup Ready soya beans, seeds that are tolerant to Monsanto's herbicide Roundup; and 'Bt' crops which are engineered to produce their own insecticide.

   In the first instance, the goal is to win a greater herbicide market share for a proprietary product; in the second, it is to boost seed sales at the cost of damaging the usefulness of 'Bt', a key pest management product relied upon by many farmers, including most organic farmers, as a powerful alternative to insecticides. These technologies respond to the need of bio-technology companies to intensify farmers' dependence upon seeds protected by so-called 'intellectual property rights', which conflict directly with the age-old rights of farmers to reproduce, share or store seeds.

3   The integration of the seed and chemical industries appears destined to accelerate increases in per acre expenditures for seeds plus chemicals, delivering significantly lower returns to growers. Companies developing herbicide tolerant crops are trying to shift as much per acre cost as possible from the

herbicide onto the seed via seed costs and/or technology charges. Increasingly price reductions for herbicides will be limited to growers purchasing technology packages. In Illinois, the adoption of herbicide-resistant crops makes for the most expensive soya bean seed-plus-weed management system in modern history – between US$40 and US$60 per acre depending on rates, weed pressure, etc. Three years ago, the average seed-plus-weed control costs on Illinois farms was US$26 per acre, and represented 23 per cent of variable costs; today they represent 35–40 per cent. Many farmers are willing to pay for the simplicity and robustness of the new weed management system, but such advantages may be short-lived as ecological problems arise.

4   Recent experimental trials have shown that genetically engineered seeds do not increase the yield of crops (see above).

5   Many scientists claim that the ingestion of genetically engineered food is harmless, but recent evidence shows that there are potential risks. The new proteins produced in such foods could themselves act as allergens or toxins that would alter the metabolism of the food-producing plant or animal. This would cause *it* to produce new allergens or toxins, or reduce its nutritional quality or value – as in the case of herbicide-resistant soya beans that contained less isoflavones, an important phytoestrogen present in soya beans which is believed to protect women from a number of cancers.

At present the markets of many developing countries importing soya beans and corn from the USA, Argentina and Brazil are being flooded by genetically engineered foods, and no one can predict the health effects on consumers, most of whom are unaware that they are eating such food. Because genetically engineered food remains unlabelled, consumers cannot discriminate between GM and non-GM food; should serious health problems arise, it will be extremely difficult to trace them to their source. Lack of labelling also helps to shield the corporations from liability.

6　Transgenic plants which produce their own insecticides closely follow the pesticide paradigm, including built-in failure due to pest resistance to insecticides. Instead of the failed 'one pest–one chemical' model, genetic engineering emphasizes a 'one pest–one gene' approach, shown over and over again in laboratory trials to fail: pest species rapidly adapt and develop resistance to the insecticide present in the plant. Not only will the new varieties fail over the short-to-medium term, despite so-called voluntary resistance management schemes, but in the process, as we have seen, they may render useless the natural pesticide 'Bt'.

7　The global fight for market share is leading companies to massively deploy transgenic crops around the world (more than 30 million hectares in 1998) without proper advance testing of short- or long-term impacts on human health and ecosystems. Many scientists are concerned that the large-scale use of transgenic crops poses a series of environmental risks; in certain conditions it produces a new viral strain with analtered host range.

8　There are many unanswered ecological questions regarding the impact of transgenic crops. Many environmental groups have argued for the creation of suitable regulation to mediate the testing and release of transgenic crops to offset environmental risks and demand a much better assessment and understanding of ecological issues associated with genetic engineering. This is crucial as many results emerging from the environmental performance of released transgenic crops suggest that, in the development of 'resistant crops', not only is there a need to test direct effects on the target insect or weed, but the indirect effects on the plant (growth, nutrient content, metabolic changes), soil, and non-target organisms. It is a tragedy in the making that so many millions of hectares have been planted without proper biosafety standards.

9　As the private sector has exerted more and more dominance in advancing new biotechnologies, the public sector has had to invest a growing share of its scarce resources in enhancing biotechnological capacities in public institutions, including the CGIAR, and in evaluating and responding to the challenges posed by incorporating private sector technologies into existing farming systems.

Civil society must request more research on alternatives to biotechnology by universities and other public organizations. There is also an urgent need to challenge the regime of patents and intellectual property rights intrinsic to the WTO, which not only provides multinational corporations with the right to seize and patent genetic resources, but will also accelerate the rate at which market forces encourage monocultural cropping with genetically uniform transgenic varieties. From the standpoint of history and ecological theory, it is not difficult to predict the negative impacts of such environmental simplification on the health of modern agriculture.

10 Although there may be some useful applications of biotechnology (such as the breeding of drought-resistant varieties or crops resistant to weed competition), because these desirable traits are polygenic and difficult to engineer, these innovations will take at least ten years to refine for field use. Once available – and if farmers can afford them – the contribution to yield enhancement of such varieties will be between 20 and 35 per cent; the rest of yield increases must come from agricultural management. Much of the needed food can be produced by small farmers located throughout the world using agro-ecological technologies (see Chapter 9).

Miguel A. Altieri, University of California, Berkeley and Peter Rosset, Food First/Institute for Food and Development Policy, Oakland, California, October 1999

CHAPTER 8

PUTTING FOOD SECURITY
INTO TRADE:
NGOS Speak

*'Business first ignores NGOs, then despises them, then reluctantly listens
to them, before finally heeding their messages'*
— Nick de Rosa, Senior Vice President,
Monsanto, at Davos 2000

One of the chief arguments of the free trade lobby is that the alternative is worse. The alternative, it maintains, is protectionism —
'and look where this led us in the 1930s — worldwide recession,
leading to the Second World War, etc. etc. Free trade is our guarantee
of a peaceful world. Without free trade, poverty and war will be our
lot.'

It is an argument based on fear and on the misrepresentation of the
views of others. There are abundantly more alternatives to unbridled
free trade than protectionism. Fear appears to be blinding free trade
advocates to the fact that among those who are putting forward alternative suggestions, almost no one wants a world where nation states
close their borders to other nations. The key question in the minds of
many non-governmental organizations is what kind of international
trade system will help the world's most vulnerable people? How can
the world trade system and the WTO contribute to food security?

The following ideas were put forward by NGOs either at or
around the time of the Seattle meeting. NGOs want international
trade to change to a fairer system. Opposition to the procedures and

the rules of the WTO is the core of their objections. Some want agri-culture to be taken out of the WTO. Such NGO ideas are important suggestions for the future of the trading system and for food security.

The following are some of the proposals put forward by the Liaison Committee of Development NGOs to the EU (NGDO–EU) in Brussels.

Fourteen development NGO recommendations

Introduction

The WTO's Agreement on Agriculture, by setting the overarching framework for agricultural trade and development, has significant implications for achieving sustainable agriculture. The Agreement's objectives of removing support and protection have not promoted the goals of sustainable agriculture and food security; nor have they ade-quately addressed the food security and agricultural development needs of developing countries. The current rules are biased towards developed countries and multinational agribusiness, and are unfair to developing countries. They allow developed countries to subsidize their domestic agriculture and exports heavily, but do not address the problem of dumping by private firms of agricultural products on world markets at less than the cost of production. The outcome is that developing countries are forced by the rules to allow the influx of sub-sidized imports, which compete unfairly with agricultural goods produced by their own farmers without benefit of subsidy. Despite a commitment to allow more market access, the rules also allow developed countries to maintain high tariffs on so-called sensitive products, which are often precisely those products of greatest export value to developing countries; as a result, the world export market share of developing countries has remained static since 1990.

The effects of subsidized exports and dumped products are to depress prices and threaten local production of food in developing countries. The rules currently require minimum access for products that are not significant imports; hence a developing country's staple crop production can be devastated by an influx of cheap imports.

WTO members have also broken their promise to assist net-food-importing developing countries financially during the adjustment process by failing to implement the Marrakech Decision.

The rules of the Agreement have operated within the following context:

- volatile world prices for primary products, with extreme highs and lows which are predicted to continue with further liberalization;
- increasing commercial imports of basic foodstuffs by least developed countries and net-food-importing developing countries, increasing their dependency and exposing them to the fluctuations of the world market;
- declining food aid, the running down of public stockholdings, and structural adjustment, reducing or eliminating domestic support for farmers;
- overproduction in the North (including the EU) compared with declining agricultural production in the LDCs;
- increasing marginalization of small-scale farmers and related livelihoods as farm-gate prices have been pushed below the cost of production;
- increasing concentration in agribusiness resulting in a lack of price transparency and the creation of cartels.

The recommendations

1 *No new negotiations before review of the Agreement on Agriculture*. Before further liberalization in agriculture takes place, we call for a meaningful official review of the Agreement, at a national and international level, with a view to removing its imbalances and unfair provisions. This should include:

- experience to date of implementation by developing countries;
- effects on agricultural trade;
- impacts on food security at the local level;
- participation of civil society;
- the costs of implementing the agreements in developing countries.

As a contribution to the review, a high-level meeting under the joint auspices of the WTO, the FAO, UNCTAD and other UN agencies should be held. Attended by governments, civil society and intergovernmental organizations, this should discuss the impact assessment of the Agreement on Agriculture. The meeting should be preceded by a series of national debates involving government and civil society. The review and the built-in agenda should consider the other recommendations listed below.

2 *Marrakech Decision to be strengthened and implemented urgently.* One reason why net-food-importing developing countries (NFIDCs) and LDCs are concerned about losing the benefits of export subsidies, and thus cheaper food, is the non-implementation of the Marrakech Decision, which has undermined the credibility of calls for another round of liberalization. It is essential to end the dependency on export subsidies as a source of cheap food, which has longer-term negative welfare effect implications. Instead, efforts must be made to enhance the food production capacity of NFIDCs and LDCs.

At the Marrakech ministerial meeting in 1994, WTO members recognized that NFIDCs and LDCs would need assistance during the liberalization process. The Decision promised financial support to ensure adequate food imports could be maintained and to improve agricultural productivity and infrastructure, together with food aid, so that the NFIDCs and LDCs were compensated for the fluctuations in market price and also to build up their self-reliance. It has never been implemented, however, despite significant fluctuations in international prices, reduction of public stockholding by some 60 per cent and a 47 per cent increase in NFIDC cereal import bills between 1993/4 and 1997/8.

Now the Marrakech Decision should be revised to incorporate:

- utilization of market-based mechanisms to automatically trigger assistance at times of high prices or low domestic production;
- assistance with regular WTO notification, remedial action within the WTO framework and use of the dispute settlement process;
- commitments for the provision of technical and financial assistance to improve agricultural productivity, facilitate agricultural development and avoid long-term dependency in LDCs and NFIDCs;

- establishment of a fund based on contributions from the major agricultural exporters to pay for the supply of staple food items to NFIDCs at concessional rates during times of high prices.

3 Creation of a Food Security Box. Food Security should have top priority in a revised Agreement on Agriculture, and should be mentioned in the preamble of the agreement as a central objective. It should be articulated further through the development of a 'Food Security Box' targeted at those developing countries who cannot invest in or subsidize agriculture but need to protect indigenous, vulnerable, small-scale producers to ensure their food security – for instance through the use of border measures. The Food Security Box, like other existing exemptions (such as the Green and Blue Boxes), would be a series of exemptions to the Agreement for developing countries whose agriculture was not meeting basic food security needs. A Food Security Box would allow developing countries and net-food-importing countries to further food security by protecting their own agricultural sectors and markets through exemptions from the WTO demands (minimum market access, tariffication/reduction of tariffs) and increasing domestic support for agriculture until they have achieved a greater level of food self-reliance.

4 An end to export subsidies and export restraints. Agriculture in developing countries is hit twice: once by subsidized overproduction in developed countries which is off-loaded onto world markets, depressing prices; and again by the provision of export subsidies, resulting at times in the sale of EU products below the cost of production or significantly more cheaply than agricultural produce from some of the poorest countries.

Export restraints can also undermine food security by promoting price variability and uncertainty. Shortages can be created artificially, raising prices and sometimes quality of imported foodstuffs. The net effect of these instruments is to undermine domestic agriculture in developing countries, to increase dependency on a 'cheap', subsidized and often unsustainable food system, and to promote unreliability and fluctuations in world markets.

5 Improve access to the markets of developed countries by developing countries.
High, complex tariffs continue to be a major barrier to market access
for developing countries. We welcome the EU initiative to zero-rate
exports from the LDCs but would also recommend the same
treatment for exports originating from small-scale farmers in developing countries in general. The EU should seek to improve and simplify
market access for agricultural exports specifically from developing
countries by urging developed country members of the WTO to
establish permanent low tariffs; to abolish quotas, seasonal restrictions
and other non-tariff barriers; and to end tariff escalation on value-
added, processed goods. The use of special safeguard provisions by
developed countries should be eliminated.

6 Penalty measures when domestic support distorts international markets. The
provisions for domestic support are largely irrelevant for most developing countries because they cannot afford to support agriculture or
have been required to decrease subsidies/support under Structural
Adjustment Programmes. Exemptions allowing domestic support to
agriculture are thus mainly utilized by the developed countries.

The exemptions need to be reviewed as they are a main cause of
over-production, dumping and world price fluctuations. Whilst
environmental and social benefits may accrue, particularly with regard
to the multifunctionality of agriculture, consideration should be given
to penalty measures that are triggered where subsidized production
displaces domestic products in developing countries or non-subsidized
exports from developing countries in third markets. Subsidies linked
directly or indirectly to production which encourage over-production
geared for export should be subject to a reduction programme or
penalty measures.

A WTO regulation for the support of small-scale, ecological and
family farmers has to be developed and implemented. Measures which
promote less intensive and more sustainable food production systems
as well as the conservation of biodiversity should also be allowed,
provided they do not imply unfair competition with farmers elsewhere.
For this purpose, the Green Box should be renegotiated.

7 Exclusion of agricultural resources from patentability within the TRIPS agreement. We consider that patents and other intellectual property rights on genetic resources for food and agriculture decrease farmers' access to seed, reduce public plant breeding, increase genetic erosion, prevent seed and plant sharing, and put poor farmers out of business. We believe that the EU should:

- support an amendment to the TRIPS agreement that would enable WTO members to exclude all genetic resources for food and agriculture from the TRIPS agreement;
- recognize the traditional knowledge, bio-innovations and practices of indigenous people and farming communities; and
- agree that the Convention on Biological Diversity take precedence over the TRIPs agreement; that the prior informed consent of peoples and communities be sought before utilization of their knowledge or plants; and that profits from any commercial exploitation be shared equitably with these communities.

8 Transboundary movement of GMOs to be addressed at the Convention on Biological Diversity. The CBD is the correct and most appropriate forum in which to agree biosafety regulations, especially as GMOs could have a profound impact on biodiversity and agriculture. Biosafety regulations must not simply facilitate trade in GM products but must be able to take into account the precautionary principle and consider the possible risks to human health and the environment; the social, economic and cultural factors; and the questions raised by scientific information. We are therefore opposed to the WTO acquiring competence in this area and urge the EU to ensure that GM issues are not negotiated in the WTO, and that a biosafety protocol is agreed within the CBD. (This recommendation was accepted at talks to negotiate the protocol in January 2000. See Chapter 7.)

9 Requirement for Anti-Dumping Provisions and Competition Policy. Dumping increasingly constricts agriculture and related industries in developing countries. For example, US-based grain companies pay US farmers less than the cost of production for their crops which are then sold on the international market at below the US domestic price, competing unfairly with developing countries' exports.

Dumping by private corporations is unregulated by international agreements. The situation is made worse by the current trend in agricultural trade of commodity companies merging with agricultural input (seed and chemical) companies to create a small number of multinational companies which buy, store, ship and process the products. The potential for abuse of their market position through monopolies and oligopolies is obvious. We therefore believe that competition policy and dumping in agriculture must be addressed in any discussions on agriculture at the WTO.

10 Recognition of the role of state trading enterprises in planning for food security needs. State trading enterprises in developing countries sometimes play an important infrastructural role in the strategic management of imports for food security; calls for their abolition could therefore have a serious impact on food security planning in some developing countries. If these enterprises are abolished, other mechanisms will need to be introduced.

11 The precautionary principle to be used at all levels of standard and rule setting. Using the precautionary principle, states should be able to take into account risks to human health, socioeconomic and cultural factors, and the available scientific information when taking decisions on whether to fix higher standards or impose import restraints.

NGOs are aware that this and the Agreement on Sanitary and Phytosanitary Measures could complicate the issue of market access for developing countries. Therefore we recommend that increased investment, technology transfer and other forms of assistance should be made available to developing country exporters to meet new standards and to address persistent problems; we also recommend increased transparency and reasonable notification time when an importing country imposes new standards or amends existing ones.

12 No abuse of the Peace Clause. The Peace Clause (see p. 46) should not be used as a form of protection by developed countries (given that it refers to policies and exemptions primarily used by them) to continue to provide high levels of support to their agricultural sector and at the same time to pursue unfair trade-distorting policies which are used to maintain or break open new markets in developing countries.

13. Capacity building for developing and least developed countries. Developing countries and LDCs should receive support from developed countries to build up their capacity to participate and negotiate, as well as to implement the Agreement on Agriculture, related agreements such as the Agreement on Sanitary and Phytosanitary Measures, and standard-setting bodies such as the Codex Alimentarius Commission. This has to be negotiated with the objective of getting serious financial contributions from all developed countries.

14. Increased civil society participation in the WTO process. There is a need for greater transparency, and to increase civil society participation in the WTO process (including the Codex Alimentarius Commission), particularly in the South.[1]

Among the clearest and most forceful NGO statements were those by Friends of the Earth, Via Campesina, a group representing indigenous peoples, Food First, CAFOD and the UK Food Group.

Friends of the Earth

'Fundamental reform (of the WTO) should begin with governmental support for the following:
- A full, thorough and measured review of the social and environmental impacts of trade liberalization.
- The introduction of binding regulations to control the activities of transnational corporations.
- A balanced investment agreement under the auspices of the UN, that addresses the legitimate fears of poorer countries and civil society.

- The removal of agriculture from the WTO in order to protect and promote the many roles of agriculture.
- Unilateral initiatives by the EU to reduce export subsidies, pay compensation to net-food-importing developing countries (as promised at the end of the Uruguay Round) and grant zero tariffs on all imports from Least Developed Countries.
- Reform of the WTO's Trade Related Intellectual Property Rights (TRIPs) agreement to remove the requirement to patent plant varieties and microbiological processes; and removal of biodiversity from the TRIPs agreement.
- A new agreement in the United Nations, to be signed by heads of state, to clarify the status of multilateral environmental agreements.
- New and substantial commitments to capacity building for developing countries.
- A review of the status of the Lomé Convention, currently being reviewed because it conflicts with WTO rules.
- A moratorium on WTO disputes relating to environment and development in the WTO and a transfer of such debates to an alternative, binding international court which does not prioritize trade over the environment.
- Increased parliamentary scrutiny of all international negotiations.
- A review of European Commission's negotiating competence in the WTO.'[2]

Via Campesina, a Worldwide Movement of Peasant and Family Farm Organizations, Statement in Seattle

'Towards an alternative to neoliberal policies and institutions such as WTO, World Bank (WB) and the IMF.

Via Campesina believes that we are experiencing a historic moment of international struggle. Massive mobilizations carried out throughout this week were the climax of years of intensive work of social movements and non-governmental organizations and they led to a near complete standstill of the WTO negotiating process. A *de facto* moratorium has now been established. Furthermore, we made an enormous leap by reaching millions of people directly and indirectly through the media with our actions. We are convinced that our resistance will continue to grow over the next years. This process is irreversible.

The governments of the main economic powers (EU, US) together with the transnational corporations (TNCs) are forcing their agenda onto peasants, farmers and indigenous communities around the world. We will never accept this arrogance.

Clearly, agriculture and food have become key issues and there is a need for profound change of the neoliberal policies and global institutions such as the WTO, IMF and WB. As a consumer leader put it: eating has become a political act. The Via Campesina adds: *producing quality products for our own people has also become a political act.*

The neo-liberal agricultural policies have led to the destruction of our family farm economies and to a profound crisis in our societies and threatens the very coherence of our societies: the right to produce our food for our own consumers, with great diversity in production and consumption according to cultural preferences. This touches our very identities as citizens of this world.

The clearest example of the violation of our identity is the fact that TNCs are imposing genetically engineered food. In a recent move the US and the EU tried to bring the discussion on bio-safety and GMOs – in essence, whether we have the right to protect ourselves against the importation of GMO products – in the WTO through a biotechnology working group. We consider this as a scandalous and provocative violation of our rights as citizens.

Via Campesina rejects the neoliberal policies that push countries into cash crop export production at the expense of domestic food production. These policies contribute to low commodity prices that are far lower than the real cost of production. Developing countries are forced to adopt these policies in order to pay their external debt. These countries must also open their borders to the importation of food which leads to even greater debt. The governments of the rich countries are giving massive subsidies without limit per farm in order to compensate price cuts and allow the TNCs to buy cheaply. This way these public funds are a direct support for industry and not for farmers. This is a vicious circle which benefits only the TNCs.

There is no doubt that the WTO is an instrument that places greater control and profits in the hands of the TNCs. The WTO is a totally inappropriate institution for democratic decision making and policy formulation on important issues such as food sovereignty, health and environmental legislation, management of genetic resources, water, forestry and land, and the organization of agricultural markets.

A profound reform of the WTO in order to make it respond to the rights and needs of people would mean the abolition of the WTO itself! We do not believe that the WTO will allow such a profound reform. Therefore, the Via Campesina, as an international movement responsible for the agricultural sector, demands that agriculture should be taken out of the WTO. Perhaps more appropriately, let's take the WTO out of agriculture. We invite other sectors to demand the same. We, as societies, must create an alternative to the current neoliberal policies and to institutions such as the WTO, WB and the IMF. We must civilize these international policies and institutions. The Via Campesina invites social movements to initiate a participatory process with national governments to further develop an alternative model. This alternative should include the following:

(1) Establish alternatives to the neoliberal policies and institu-

tions such as the WTO, WB and the IMF. (2) Continue to mobilize public opinion to pressure TNCs and large trading powers. (3) Strengthen the UN and develop new instruments within the UN system to increase transparency and democratic control. These institutions should represent the priorities and needs of people and ensure food security and fair trade.

The Via Campesina has the following demands:

- An immediate moratorium on further WTO negotiations. This includes all discussion on agreements on investment.

- To immediately cancel the obligation of accepting the minimum importation of 5 per cent of internal consumption. All compulsory market access clauses must be cancelled.

- An evaluation of the impacts of the Marrakech agreement and an immediate correction of existing injustices.

- To remove all negotiation in the areas of food production and marketing from the WTO and from all regional and bilateral agreements.

- To create genuine international democratic mechanisms to regulate food trade while respecting food sovereignty in each country.

- To secure food sovereignty in each and every country, giving priority to food production for its people, social aspects and environment.

- To give each country the right to define their own agricultural policies in order to meet their internal needs. This includes the right to prohibit imports in order to protect domestic production and to implement agrarian reform providing peasants and small to medium-sized producers with access to land.

- To stop all forms of dumping. To protect the production of staple domestic foods.

- To prohibit biopiracy and patents on life (animal, plants, parts of the human body) including the development of sterile varieties through genetic engineering.

- To allow countries the right to establish food quality criteria appropriate to the preference of its people.

Via Campesina wants to support the International Tribunal of Peoples that has to judge the crimes committed against farming and indigenous communities. Via Campesina calls upon international and national movements, and non-governmental organizations to build strong alliances to continue to fight these neo-liberal policies and to build alternatives. If we continue to work together we will succeed! Let's globalize the struggle; let's globalize hope. **'**[3]

Proposals on TRIPs by Indigenous Peoples from Various Regions

' The TRIPs Agreement should be amended to categorically disallow the patenting of life forms.

- It should clearly prohibit the patenting of micro-organisms, plants, animals, including all their parts, whether they are genes, gene sequences, cells, cell lines, proteins, or seeds.
- It should also prohibit the patenting of natural processes, whether these are biological or microbiological, involving the use of plants, animals and micro-organisms and their parts in producing variations of plants, animals and micro-organisms.
- It should ensure the exploration and development of alternative forms of protection outside of the dominant Western intellectual property rights regime. Such alternatives must protect the knowledge and innovations and practices in agriculture, health care, and conservation of biodiversity, and

should build upon indigenous methods and customary laws protecting knowledge, heritage and biological resources.

- It should ensure that the protection offered to indigenous and traditional knowledge, innovation and practices is consistent with the Convention on Biological Diversity and the International Undertaking on Plant Genetic Resources.
- It should allow for the right of indigenous peoples and farmers to continue their traditional practices of saving, sharing and exchanging seeds, and cultivating, harvesting and using medicinal plants.
- It should prohibit scientific researchers and corporations from appropriating and patenting indigenous seeds, medicinal plants, and related knowledge about these life forms. The principles of prior informed consent and right of veto by indigenous peoples should be respected.' [4]

Food First (US-based NGO)

'We are not just against something. We know what we're fighting for – for one world with room for many worlds. WTO trade agreements, by contrast, force uniformity and lack of diversity on everybody. Every country should have the right to decide their own solutions. We will never have a socially just agriculture without fair and equitable access to land for all. A living wage and dignified conditions for farm workers are minimum requirements.' [5]

CAFOD (UK-based Aid Agency)

'The EU and US governments should now acknowledge that the atmosphere of recrimination and distrust so evident in Seattle shows the need for a thorough overhaul of the WTO, not least to ensure that developing countries are no longer sidelined within the organization.

However, the WTO's problems go much deeper than questions of organizational mechanics. They also include the organization's assumptions, aims and governance. The WTO has hitherto been seen as taking precedence among international bodies on trade-related issues. This has led to decisions which clearly affect other areas, such as environment or development (notoriously the ruling on the EU banana regime), being taken by the WTO on the basis of trade concerns alone. Other organizations and regimes (for example the new Lomé agreement) are then expected to become "WTO-compatible".

Instead, the WTO should be made "development compatible" by subordinating it to the UN system to which it theoretically belongs. When disputes arise which involve the environment, development, or other non-trade concerns, the WTO should defer to the relevant specialist agencies of the UN. Mechanisms should be put in place to enable these bodies to arbitrate fairly and quickly in disputes.

The WTO should follow the lead offered by the World Bank and IMF in recent years, and publicly commit itself to the International Development Targets, making the reduction and elimination of poverty its overriding goal. Too often, trade liberalization is seen as an end in itself, rather than as a means to the end of sustainable development. This means that, in cases where trade liberalization can actually damage development, trade liberalization comes first. One useful reform would be to overhaul the WTO's Trade Policy Review Mechanism, which reports on individual members' trade policies. This currently only reports on steps to liberalize trade, and ignores issues such as the social and environmental impact of such policies.

There is clearly a need for reform of the WTO's decision-making structures. Its insistence on taking all decisions by consensus appears superficially democratic since it gives the smallest countries the same weight as the largest. In practice, however, it has created a byzantine and opaque process of decision making which favours bilateral horsetrading between powerful nations and blocs. The real decisions are taken behind closed doors and the less powerful nations are cajoled or coerced into agreement.

The general call for increased transparency at the WTO should include the role of transnational corporations, which maintain an effective lobby in Geneva and drafted many of the agreements in the Uruguay Round process. CAFOD does not oppose the involvement of business in the WTO, but believes that their participation should be properly regulated, with disclosure of their finances, staff and activities in Geneva and within the WTO in general, and rules to avoid conflicts of interest arising.' [6]

UK Food Group, a Network of UK-based NGOs

'Current trade liberalization is pressurizing Southern countries to intensify their agriculture, producing a bias against small farmers in favour of larger producers, agribusiness and export crop production. Transnational agribusiness corporations have reaped the gains from trade liberalization, and have become even more powerful.

Trade liberalization has thus been accompanied by growing land alienation, declining food entitlements, a growing number of hungry people, and erosion of agricultural biodiversity. The

UK Food Group calls for the institutionalization of food security within the Agreement on Agriculture; this requires addressing a number of broad areas, including reducing the impact of Northern subsidies on Southern agriculture, improving access for developing country exports to Northern markets, meaningful special and differential treatment for developing countries and implementation of the Marrakech Ministerial Decision.[97]

Footnote: the need to discriminate

The huge NGO turnout for meetings, demonstrations and advocacy work in Seattle showed the depth of concern about WTO issues. NGOs exposed flaws in the WTO system and pointed to changes that could bring benefits, making the system work in the broader public and global interest, including food security. There was a widespread feeling among NGOs that both trade and the WTO are too dominant and that this must change. For this to happen, however, a key principle on which WTO rules are based has to change – the principle of non-discrimination. This states that the trading system 'should be without discrimination – a country should not discriminate between its trading partners and it should not discriminate between its own and foreign products, services or nationals'.

This principle is basically unjust – anti-democratic, because it threatens laws drawn up by democratically elected governments, and anti-development in that it ties the hands of developing countries, making development policy subservient to trade policy. It reduces the freedom of governments to stipulate that locally produced foodstuffs and materials are used. Application of the principle leads to a bizarre situation in which 'free trade' means less freedom of manoeuvre. National laws that stand in the way of this principle have to be revoked.

The non-discrimination principle pitches the weakest countries into the same economic stream as the strongest countries. It is arguably sound for industrialized countries at a similar stage of economic development. But when applied to countries at very different levels of development, the stronger country is likely to gain at the expense of the weaker, which is the complaint of the NGOs as well as the vast majority of developing country governments. 'When countries or people are unequal, treating them the same leads to more inequality.'[8]

If a new WTO round is ever launched, and if it is to be a development round as suggested by developing countries, then the rules and principles of the WTO that stand in the way of development and food security need to be revised. Developing countries should be allowed to discriminate in favour of their domestic interests if this assists economic, social and human development. Governments and business need to heed and act on the message of the NGOs.

Why Reform of the WTO Is the Wrong Agenda

Walden Bello, Focus on the Global South (an autonomous programme of policy research and action of the Chulalongkorn University Social Research Institute, Bangkok).

In the wake of the collapse of the Seattle meeting, there has emerged the opinion that reform of the WTO is the programme that NGOs, governments, and citizens must embrace. The collapse is said to provide a unique window of opportunity for a reform agenda.

But is the WTO necessary? This is the fundamental question on which the question of reform hinges. World trade did not need the WTO to expand 17-fold between 1948 and 1997, from US$124 billion to US$10,772 billion. This expansion took place under the flexible GATT trade regime. The WTO's founding in 1995 did not respond to a collapse or crisis of world trade such as happened in the 1930s. It was not necessary for global peace, since no world war or trade-related war had taken place during that period. GATT was, in fact, functioning reasonably well as a framework for liberalising world trade. Its dispute settlement system was flexible and with its recognition of the 'special and differential status' of developing countries it provided the space in a global economy for Third World countries to use trade policy for development and industrialization. The WTO is necessary to the United States but not to the rest of the world. The 'necessity' of the WTO is one of the biggest lies of our time.

Reform is a viable strategy when the system in question is fundamentally fair but has simply been corrupted, as happens in some democracies. It is not a viable strategy when a system is as fundamentally unequal in purposes, principles, and processes as the WTO. The WTO systematically protects the trade and economic advantages of the rich countries, particularly the United States. It is based on a paradigm or philosophy that denigrates the right to take activist measures to achieve development on the part of less developed countries, thus leading to a radical dilution of their right to 'special and differential treatment'. The WTO raises inequality into a principle of decision making.

The WTO is often promoted as a 'rules-based' trading framework that protects the weaker and poorer countries from unilateral actions by the stronger states. The opposite is true: the WTO, like many other multilateral international agreements, is meant to institutionalize and legitimize inequality. Its main purpose is to reduce the tremendous policing costs that would have to be met if the stronger powers were involved in disciplining many small countries in a more fluid, less structured international system.

It is not surprising that both the WTO and the IMF are currently mired in a severe crisis of legitimacy. For both are highly centralized, highly unaccountable, highly non-transparent global institutions that seek to subjugate, control or harness vast swathes of global economic, social, political and environmental processes to the needs and interests of a global minority of states, elites, and TNCs.

The dynamics of such institutions clash with the burgeoning democratic aspirations of peoples, countries, and communities in both the North and the South. The centralizing dynamics of these institutions clash with the efforts of communities and nations to regain control of their fate and achieve a modicum of security by reconcentrating and decentralizing economic and political power. In other words, these are Jurassic institutions in an age of participatory political and economic democracy.

Developing country governments and international civil society must not allow their energies to be hijacked into reforming these institutions. This will only amount to administering a facelift to fundamentally flawed institutions. Indeed, today's need is not another centralized global institution, reformed or unreformed, but the deconcentration and decentralization of institutional power and the creation of a pluralistic system of institutions and organizations interacting with one another amidst broadly defined and flexible agreements and understandings.

It was under such a more pluralistic global system, where hegemonic power was still far from institutionalized in a set of all-encompassing and powerful multilateral organizations, that the Latin American and many Asian countries were able to achieve a modicum of industrial development in the period 1950–70. It was under a more pluralistic world system, under a GATT that was limited in its power, flexible, and more sympathetic to the special status of developing countries, that the East and Southeast Asian countries were able to become newly industrializing countries through activist state trade and industrial policies that departed significantly from the free-market biases enshrined in the WTO.

The alternative to a powerful WTO is not a Hobbesian state of nature. It is always the powerful that have stoked this fear. The reality of international economic relations in a world marked by a multiplicity of international and regional institutions that check one another is a far cry from the propaganda image of a 'nasty' and 'brutish' world. Of course, the threat of unilateral action by the powerful is ever present in such a system, but it is one that even the powerful hesitate to fulfil for fear of its consequences on their legitimacy as well as the reaction it would provoke in the form of opposing coalitions.

In other words, what developing countries and international civil society should aim at is not to reform the WTO but, through a combination of passive and active measures, to radically reduce its power and to make it simply another international institution coexisting with and being checked by other international organizations, agreements, and regional groupings. These would include such diverse actors and institutions as UNCTAD, multilateral environmental agreements, the ILO and evolving trade blocs such as Mercosur in Latin America, the South Asian Association for Regional Cooperation (SAARC), the Southern African Development Community (SADC) and ASEAN in Southeast Asia. It is in such a more fluid, less structured, more pluralistic world with multiple checks and balances that the nations and communities of the South will be able to carve out the space to develop based on their values, their rhythms and the strategies of their choice.[9]

CHAPTER 9

CONCLUSION
Food security with less trade?

'You see these things differently if you come from a developing country'
– Neth Dano, Searice (NGO), Philippines

'The industrial model of agriculture has failed miserably to feed the world'
– Anne Schwartz, organic farmer, Saskatchewan, Canada

It is time to think the unthinkable. The stark question is whether food security could be better advanced with less trade, rather than with more trade. Should governments of developing countries put more resources into achieving food security and give less priority to trade?

The more 'thinkable' question is whether the nature of trade liberalization can change to help food security. It is certainly the case that 'a more level playing field' on liberalization would help developing countries. If, for example, the European Union were to abolish the Common Agricultural Policy, its market would be more open to Third World foodstuffs, as discussed in Chapter 3 – although this would be likely to make only a small contribution to food security for the poorest people. The 'unthinkable', therefore, needs to be examined.

Despite all the problems outlined in Chapter 2, food security is advancing in a number of developing countries for reasons that have nothing to do with trade. In at least one country, Cuba, it is progressing because of restraints on trade. In many developing countries, resource-poor farmers are increasing their crop yields, at low cost, by using few external inputs and by integrating traditional technologies. These farmers are already making a significant contribution to food security at household, national and regional levels in Africa, Asia and Latin America. Their experience shows that more food can be produced if appropriate technologies are used.

'Quietly, slowly and very significantly, sustainable agriculture is sweeping the farming systems of the world,' says Jules Pretty of the Centre for Environment and Society at the University of Essex; 'we have reached a turning point in agricultural development. We now realize that there are ways of increasing food production on existing land.'[1]

Yields are increasing and being sustained by using technological approaches that are based on agroecological principles which emphasize diversity, synergy, recycling and integration, community participation and empowerment. As well as yield increases, biodiversity is being conserved and soil fertility restored.

The countries that have made important breakthroughs in the task of achieving food security in recent years have done so largely through the use of low-cost, appropriate technologies. In Mali and Burkina Faso, for example, widespread deployment of new water-harvesting techniques has allowed farmers to make better use of rainfall. 'This has substantially increased food production. The average household in countries like this had a food deficit of around 150 kilos a year at the beginning of the 1990s. They are now producing on average a surplus of 600 kilos a year.'[2]

This massive turnaround has come about partly because of community organization and farmers learning to work together, 'but it's also about governments realizing that if you create the right conditions, this allows people to make a big jump in terms of their productivity. This offers great hope.'[3]

Sustainable agriculture – farming that makes the best use of nature's goods and services, whilst not damaging the environment – can be achieved by integrating natural processes such as nutrient cycling, nitrogen fixation, soil regeneration and pest predators into food production processes. It minimizes the use of non-renewable inputs (pesticides and fertilizers) that damage the environment or harm the health of farmers or consumers, and makes better use of the knowledge and skills of farmers, so improving their self-reliance and capacities.

The challenge for sustainable agriculture, Jules Pretty believes, 'is to maximize the use of locally available and renewable resources'.[4] He points to impressive increases in crop outputs that are coming from this method of agriculture. Some 223,000 farmers in southern Brazil, for example, who are using green manures and carefully integrating livestock into their system, have doubled their yields of wheat and maize. By using a range of soil and water management technologies, more than 300,000 farmers in southern and western India have tripled their sorghum and millet yields, while 200,000 farmers across Kenya have used similar technologies to double their maize yields. Using regenerative technologies, around 45,000 farmers in Guatemala and Honduras have increased their yields of maize so much as to encourage remigration back from the cities. As for biotechnology, Pretty points out that 'this is not currently a necessary precondition for feeding the world'.

In its most recent study, the Centre for Environment and Society looked at the 45 sustainable agriculture projects and initiatives in 17 African countries and found that some 730,000 households have substantially improved food production and household food security. In 95 per cent of the projects, cereal yields have improved by 50–100 per cent, and overall food production has increased. 'The additional positive impacts on natural, social and human capital are also helping to build the assets base so as to sustain these improvements in the future.'[5]

Permaculture

Food output can be increased substantially by the use of permaculture methods. Trade has no role in permaculture; at its most basic, the concept is short for 'permanent agriculture' but it means more besides – it is concerned, for example, with sustainable energy use. Since the idea was developed in Australia in the late 1970s by agronomist/ ecologist Bill Mollison, over a hundred permaculture training institutes have been established in developing countries. Some governments, Thailand and Vietnam, for example, have set up permaculture training institutes as part of their agricultural outreach work. Permaculture is knowledge-intensive and training is therefore needed.

Farmers who practise permaculture normally use no outside inputs. And yet their crop yields can be several times higher than with chemical farming.

> Farmers who switch to permaculture methods may go through a temporary dip in yields, but eventually they should produce much more. There may be a five-year changeover time. Farmers can often achieve a four-fold increase in yields and sometimes even more. They then need only a quarter of the land to get the same yield; they can use the other three-quarters of their land for rainfall harvesting – and it is on this land that farmers can devise systems of forestry which are very high-nutrient. And the farmer is then in a pretty steady situation, getting much higher yields with no chemical fertilizer or pesticide and with no pest problems. As yields increase, so do the farmer's net profits because inputs have been reduced.[6]

Mollison cites India as perhaps the best example of where farmers increased their yields when they switched to permaculture. He recalls a course he taught north of Hyderabad for the Permaculture Institute of India: 'the people had eroded land with no soil. Now it is very productive with thousands of trees growing. We dug holes in the laterite and filled them with hay and buffalo manure and planted bananas. The Institute has gone on from there to work in 120 villages'.

> What differentiates permaculture is that it starts with an ethic of earth care, stresses people care, and goes on to say that you shall reinvest anything that you make surplus to your needs back into people and the earth. What is worrying today is that the ethical care of the earth does not appear in the ethics of charities or in education. That's why you can go and wipe out a forest and put it under the monoculture of soybeans or something, because you don't give a damn about the earth. But that phase may be coming catastrophically to an end.

Organic agriculture is not enough on its own, Mollison believes:

> you can farm organically in the sense that you don't use persistent

biocides or nitrates and still erode your land. The only thing you are caring for, perhaps, is soils. But I have seen organic farms which are heavily eroded. Organic agriculture does not necessarily relate components to each other, it takes no notice of the energy it uses. Organic farmers can build idiotic houses, for example, that use up more energy than those same farmers produce in food. The fanatical organic farmer might have seaweed transported from thousands of miles away.

Permaculture is most spectacular in very arid areas; in some areas with eroded sand dunes, for example, we have built productive organic gardens. Our institutes in Botswana and Zimbabwe are doing marvellously. The world's best dryland gardeners are the tribal people of the area. Permaculture is growing fastest wherever our teachers have been and left a core of students, some of whom become teachers.

Permaculture can make a contribution to anyone growing food if they take notice of it and use it. And people are doing this, on farms, villages, cities, suburbs, etc., in industrial and developing countries. Permaculture institutes have helped hundreds of thousands of people to become interested and involved in this. We have to remember that in much of the Third World an 'emergency' has existed for a long time, exacerbated by the greed of the West, particularly because of foreign debt, but more specifically because of the ignorance of the large aid organizations, who have helped to desertify vast areas, but done little for the poor.

I see a good chance for people who are taking permaculture seriously. By the year 2000, permaculture will be one of the very few things for people to build onto. I hope that irresponsible systems collapse sooner rather than later; the longer they survive the more damage they do. What we are doing in permaculture institutes is restating information that works, based on thousands of trials and examples. Principles drawn from these make a unique solution. Yet there is a danger that traditional knowledge will die out and that there will be no one left to work the land in a sustainable way. So let's recognize that we are in a real emergency; scientists looking at whole systems long ago recognized that. It's now so critical we should seize the television and give everybody a permaculture course for a month, so that the whole world knows how to design sustainable systems.

Pesticide reductions

Rice farmers in over 8,000 Asian villages, notably in Bangladesh, Indonesia, the Philippines and Vietnam, have reduced their use of insecticide while increasing their crop yields. In the Philippines, a participatory research study carried out by the International Rice Research Institute, the FAO and other organizations has shown that farmers who apply less pesticide than neighbouring farmers can harvest more rice from their land.

The study was carried out in the province of Nueva Ecija in central Luxon and involved three villages. The province is one the country's major irrigated rice areas, known as 'the rice bowl of the Philippines'. Ninety farmers were asked to join in the full study, 30 each from three villages, with an average landholding of just over two hectares.

In one village, La Torre, 30 farmers agreed not to apply insecticides for at least 40 days after planting their crop. The normal growing season is between 110 and 120 days. Farmers in this group had been accustomed to making two, three or more insecticide applications during the cropping season, mostly in the first 40 days after planting, to control insects such as rice green leafhopper, rice zigzag leafhoppers and the brown planthopper.

In the nearby village of Matingkis, a second group of 30 farmers had attended an FAO training course on integrated pest management techniques (IPM). With IPM, farmers control pests with a combination of cultural, plant resistance, biological and chemical control methods. These farmers also applied no insecticide for at least the first 40 days after planting. Finally, in Santo Rosario village, 30 farmers carried on with their usual pest control methods, applying their customary applications. Most farmers in the three villages plant the same rice variety, one with a good resistance to pests.

When the rice was harvested, yields averaging around 4.5 tons per hectare were reported by farmers in all three groups, with IPM-trained farmers in Matingkis having a slight edge. Farmers in Santo Rosario who sprayed insecticide fared no better than farmers who spent nothing on insecticide. But some farmers in La Torre and Matingkis, who did not spray, increased their yields, while others were thankful they did not have to spend as much on insecticide. 'At first we didn't believe that no spraying was possible without experiencing 30 per cent yield loss,' said a Matingkis farmer.

By not using insecticides, farmers saved 1,200–1,500 pesos (£30–37) over the season – a significant amount, since the average net income per hectare per season is about £100. The extra output meant they had more rice to eat or to sell. Some were persuaded beyond the confines of the project and stopped spraying altogether, not just in the first 40 days but over the entire growing season. Insecticide sales in La Torre and Matingkis villages slumped so heavily that cooperatives dropped them from their shelves.[7]

Brazil

While more than 30 million Brazilians are chronically hungry, the country could eradicate hunger in less than four years if the government gave it more priority, believes Flavio Valente, general coordinator of the Association of Projects Fighting Hunger. International trade would have little part to play. 'Anti-hunger organizations and movements in Brazil, in many places in partnership with governmental agencies, have demonstrated, in practice, how hunger can be overcome in a short period of time, with very simple actions with the use of existing technical, human, material and economic resources.' A number of microcredit and minimum-income strategies at local, state and national level have been very successful, and a fall in the prevalence of malnutrition has been observed 'in a very short period of time', says Valente.[8]

A school feeding programme is reaching 30 million Brazilian children daily and has stimulated the purchase of food from local producers. A programme for malnourished mothers and infants distributes milk and oil to more than two million beneficiaries; another distributes nearly two million food baskets a month to the poorest families in 1,200 poor areas of Brazil.

In parts of Brazil where landless people have been given land, a transformation has occurred. For example in the village of Pedra Vermelha, in the northeast, people were given government-owned land after camping by an adjacent roadside for a year. Four years later, corn, fruit and vegetables are plentiful and 'Pedra Vermelha is a picture of rural prosperity,' says Clive Robinson of Christian Aid.[9]

Beneficiaries of land reform in Brazil have an annual income equivalent to 3.7 minimum wages, while still landless labourers average only 0.7 of the minimum. Infant mortality among families of beneficiaries has dropped to only half of the national average. 'This provides a powerful argument that using land reform to create a small farm economy is not only good for local economic development, but is also more effective social policy than allowing business-as-usual to keep driving the poor out of rural areas and into burgeoning cities.'[10]

Cuba

The recent history of Cuba provides a vivid illustration of what can happen when a country trades less. A trade embargo of Cuba, imposed by the United States, plus the collapse of the island's sugar exports to the former Soviet Union, led to a switch to farming based on low external inputs, and especially to organic agriculture, that has advanced food security. Cuba 'has found it virtually impossible to import the chemicals and machinery necessary to practice modern, intensive agriculture. Instead, it has turned to farming much of its land organically – with results that overturn the myths about the inefficiency of organic farming,' says Hugh Warwick.[11]

The crash in agricultural imports led to a general diversification within farming on the island. 'Oxen are being bred to replace tractors; integrated pest management is being developed to replace pesticides no longer available; the promotion of better cooperation among farmers both within and between communities is promoted; and the rural exodus of previous decades is being reversed by encouraging people to remain in rural areas.'

The most significant aspect has been the removal of the chemical crutch, as imports of inputs such as pesticides and herbicides dried up. Cuba was well placed to respond to this; while it has only 2 per cent of the Caribbean's population, it has some 11 per cent of its scientists. 'And many of them, influenced by the ecology movement, had already developed a critique of Cuba's intensive agriculture system They had also begun to develop alternatives to chemical dependency, which have since come into their own.' Cuba has begun to develop a biological pest-control programme – farmers are producing biocontrol agents instead of pesticides to protect their crops.

As a result of such necessary innovations, the Cuban landscape, once dominated by chemical inputs, has changed rapidly. And many of the new control methods are proving more efficient than pesticides. For example, the use of cut banana stems baited with honey to attract ants, which are then placed in sweet potato fields, has led to the complete control of the sweet potato borer – a major pest – by the predatory ants. According to Hugh Warwick,

> Crop rotations, green manuring, intercropping and soil conservation are all common today. Planners have also sought to encourage urbanites to move to the countryside, as labour for alternative agriculture is now a constraint on its growth (organic farming is generally more labour-intensive than chemical farming). Programmes are now aiming to create more attractive housing in the countryside, supplemented with services, and to encourage urban people to work on farms for periods of two weeks to two years.
>
> Conventional wisdom has it that a switch away from chemically intensive agriculture will ultimately lead to a fall in yields – though this is not necessarily the case. In Cuba, the intensive state sector, controlling the vast majority of the land, suffered a fall in yields, but small-scale farmers were able in some instances to increase their productivity. In many cases, peasant farmers had remembered old methods and reapplied them.

Warwick also draws on the experience of Peter Rosset:

> In almost every case they said they had done two things: remembered the old techniques – like intercropping and manuring – that their parents and grandparents had used before the advent of modern chemicals, simultaneously incorporating input-substituting bio-pesticides and bio-fertilizers into their production practices. Incidentally, many of them commented on the noticeable drop in acute pesticide poisoning incidents on their crops since 1989.[12]

Urban agriculture has also been one of the solutions. The capital Havana has 20 per cent of Cuba's population, some 2.5 million people. Feeding them was clearly a priority. Prior to 1989, urban agriculture was virtually unheard of, but by 1998, with government encouragement, there were officially recognized 'gardens' in Havana, cultivated by over 30,000 people, covering some 30 per cent of the available land.

In October 1999 the Grupo de Agricultura Organica (GAO), the Cuban organic farming association at the forefront of the transition to organic agriculture, received the Right Livelihood Award – the 'Alternative Nobel Prize' – which honours outstanding contributions to building a better world.

Fair trade

Food security would be advanced by an increase in fair trade arrangements. Under fair trade, the actual producers receive a higher return than under conventional trade, a return that gives them the opportunity of becoming food secure. The coffee trade provides a good example. With sales of around US$8 billion a year, it is the world's most valuable traded primary commodity after oil, providing employment for more than 25 million people in some 80 countries. Around 70 per cent of coffee growers are small farmers who grow the crop in the hope of a cash income. But their share of the price that coffee fetches on world markets is often well below the cost of production. A sustained period of low prices during the first half of the 1990s left many growers bankrupt and destitute; some lost their land, while others neglected their crop to get casual jobs. Coffee harvests declined in quality as a result.

The problem for the grower is not just that world coffee prices are low or even that they fluctuate widely. The deeper problem lies in the workings of the world coffee market. Most coffee is traded down a line of dealers before it is exported – it can change hands as many as 150 times, leaving growers with a meagre return even when prices rise. But some growers are shielded from this system. They are members of farmers' organizations which sell directly to coffee-roasting companies who comply with internationally accepted fair trade criteria and have the Fairtrade Mark. This allows farmers to produce coffee in a way that gives them a fair return, is socially and environmentally sustainable and allows them to invest in improvements.

The mark was established by the Fairtrade Foundation, set up in 1993 by NGOs, including the World Development Movement and Christian Aid, to help Third World producers of coffee, cocoa, bananas, tea and honey to receive a fair share of their trade. The Fairtrade Mark is awarded as a seal of approval to products which are traded fairly. The difference between Fairtrade and conventional coffee is that it must be bought direct from small grower organizations. These must be genuinely representative of their members; there must also be advance payment to ensure that the grower organization can finance itself. Fairtrade coffees are independently audited and guaranteed to meet these criteria.

Growth is phenomenal – sales of Fairtrade coffee in the UK, for example, grew by over 50 per cent a year in the late 1990s; their wholesale value in 1998 was £8.2 million ($12.4 million). In terms of value, fairly traded ground coffees now have 7.5 per cent of the UK coffee market. Under the Fairtrade system, farmers' organizations receive a guaranteed price which covers the cost of production and allows for investment and a basic living wage. When coffee prices are low, the Fairtrade price can be double the world price. When prices are higher, farmers receive 5 cents per pound more, which goes directly to the farmers' organizations.

> More important than the price, perhaps, is the direct nature of the trading relationship. Fairtrade terms also mean long-term contracts under which growers receive advance payments of up to 60 per cent.[13]

By the end of the 1990s, around 510,000 small-scale coffee growers were members of producer groups which are registered with a Bonn-based organization, FairTrade Labelling Organizations International (FLO-International). With 16 member organizations in Western Europe, North America and Japan that have broadly similar aims to the Fairtrade Foundation, FLO-International has 186 coffee producer groups on its register, mostly with between 100 to 500 members.

The balance of the evidence

There are many examples of how high crop yields can be obtained and sustained from agriculture with low external inputs – or, as in the case of permaculture, with no external inputs at all. These examples owe nothing to international trade. But farmers are closer to the problems than policy makers.

> Policy makers believe that the answer is in developing and promoting free market systems for agricultural produce.... Rural people have articulated their problems rather differently. They have given highest priority to their agricultural production problems, very often related to staple crops, and marketing problems have occurred much further down the list. The overwhelming evidence is that rural people are aware of simple methods and technologies to increase their production, but they are frustrated in their attempts to do so because of lack of means to acquire them.[14]

Food security can be achieved, even in the world's poorest countries, if policy makers will examine the evidence and take the right measures. 'It is certainly possible to eliminate hunger in Africa, since the continent's resources far exceed actual needs,' says a UN International Fund for Agricultural Development official.[15]

This highlights a key factor. Resources in many 'poor' countries are relatively abundant; food grows well, yet 800 million people are hungry. They are being criminally let down by both their national governments and the international economic system. Academics and NGOs are not sufficiently addressing central questions such as – why should developing countries export food to the West when their own populations are experiencing hunger? Are they wise to use so much of their best land to feed the well-fed in the West? Is the whole thing out of balance – are developing countries placing too much reliance on trade?

International trade has a role to play in food security efforts, but it needs to be less dominant and better balanced with other policy instruments. Trade rules should not oblige countries to make other policies subservient to trade. With the advent of structural adjustment programmes in the early 1980s, governments of developing countries were coerced into making trade too dominant; this often came at the expense of food production for domestic consumption and of efforts to overcome poverty.

Structural adjustment programmes hid the fact that in the final analysis, countries don't trade, companies do. And the interests of transnational corporations sit uneasily with those of food security and anti-poverty efforts. Governments have to decide whether to put more emphasis on food for their people or trade for the corporations. Trade needs to be more participatory, democratic and fair – and that makes it difficult to envisage much of a role for the large corporations or for the WTO in its present form.

Overcoming poverty and ensuring food for all deserve to become central to international concern and attention. All policy, including trade policy, must reflect this concern.

RECOMMENDED
FURTHER READING

Christian Aid, *Fair Shares: Transnational Companies, the WTO and the World's Poorest Communities*, London: Christian Aid, 1999.

—, *Selling Suicide*, London: Christian Aid, 1999.

International Cooperation for Development and Solidarity (CIDSE), *Patenting of Life, the Poor and Food Security*, Brussels: CIDSE, 1999.

Kneen, B., *Invisible Giant*, London: Pluto Press, 1996.

Madeley, J., *Big Business, Poor Peoples*, Zed Books, 1999.

Moore Lappé, F., J. Collins and P. Rosset, *World Hunger: Twelve Myths*, London: Earthscan, 1988.

Murphy, S., *Trade and Food Security. An Assessment of the Uruguay Round Agreement on Agriculture*, London: CIIR, 1999.

Oxfam, *Genetically Modified Crops, World Trade and Food Security*, Oxford: Oxfam, 1999.

Pretty, J., *Splice*, August/September 1998.

Sharma, D., *GATT to WTO: Seeds of Despair*, New Delhi: Konark Publishers, 1995.

UK Food Group, *Hungry for Power*, London: UK Food Group, 1999.

Warwick, H., 'Cuba's Organic Revolution', *The Ecologist*, Vol. 29, No. 8 (December 1999).

SOURCES

Action Aid, *Crops and Robbers: Biopiracy and the Patenting of Staple Food Crops*, London: Action Aid, 1999.

——, *TRIPs and Farmers' Rights*, London: Action Aid, 1999.

Africa Watch, *Africa Recovery*, New York: United Nations, 1998.

'America Backs Down on GM foods', *The Observer*, 30 January 2000.

Association of World Council of Churches-related Development Organizations, *Brussels Blind Spot*, Brussels: APRODEV, 1999.

'Bean Counting in Chile', *The World Paper*, Boston: December 1993.

'Biodiversity in Agriculture: Policy Issues', *ILEIA Newsletter*, Leusden, Netherlands, 1999.

Blench, R., *Seasonal Climatic Forecasting*, London: Overseas Development Institute, 1999.

Bread for the World Institute, *Hunger 2000. A Program to End Hunger*, Silver Spring, Maryland, US: Bread for the World Institute, 2000.

Bundell, K. and E. Maybin, *After the Prawn Rush*, London: Christian Aid, 1996.

Bussolo, M. and H-B. Solignac Lecomte, *Trade Liberalisation and Poverty*, London: Overseas Development Institute, 1999.

Chisvo, M., *Trade Liberalisation and Household Food Security: a Study from Zimbabwe*, London: CIIR, 2000.

Christian Aid, *Fair Shares: Transnational Companies, the WTO and the World's Poorest Communities*, London: Christian Aid, 1999.

——, *Selling Suicide*, London: Christian Aid, 1999.

CIDSE, *Patenting of Life, the Poor and Food Security*, Brussels: CIDSE, 1999.

Crucible Group, *Peoples, Plants and Patents*, Canada: International Development Research Centre, 1994.

Davies, S. *Adaptable Livelihoods, Coping with Food Insecurity in the Malian Sahel*, Basingstoke: MacMillan, 1996.

European Commission, 'Future ACP Trade', *The Courier*, October/November 1999, Brussels: European Commission.

Food and Agriculture Organization, *The State of Food Insecurity in the World 1999*, Rome: FAO, October 1999.

George, Susan, *The Lugano Report*, London: Pluto, 1999.

Hinrichsen, D. and J. Rowley, 'A Look into the Future World of 8 Billion Humans', *People & the Planet*, Vol. 8, No. 4 (1999).

International Agricultural Development magazine, July/August 1998.

——, November/December 1999.

International Federation of Red Cross and Red Crescent Societies, *World Disasters Report*, Oxford: International Federation of Red Cross and Red Crescent Societies/ OUP, 1996.

——, *World Disasters Report*, Oxford: International Federation of Red Cross and Red Crescent Societies/OUP, Oxford, 1999.

International Food Policy Food Research Institute, *Nutrient Depletion in the Agricultural Soils of Africa*, Washington: October 1999.

James, H. 'Is Liberalization Reversible?', *Finance & Development*, December 1999, Washington: International Monetary Fund.

Kemp, J., 'Third Way Route Jams Trade', *Financial Times*, 2 August 1999.

Khor, M., 'Take Care, the WTO Majority is Tired of Being Manipulated', *International Herald Tribune*, 21 December 1999.

Kneen, B., *Invisible Giant*, London: Pluto Press, 1996.

Lundberg, M. and B. Milanovic, 'The Truth about Global Inequality', *Financial Times*, 25 February 2000.

Madeley, J. (ed.), *Trade and the Hungry: How International Trade Is Causing Hunger*, Brussels: Association of World Council of Churches-related Development Organizations, 1999.

Madeley, J., *Big Business, Poor Peoples*, Zed Books, 1999.

'Meeting Needs of Developing Countries', *Financial Times*, 12 August 1999.

Ministry of Agriculture, Fisheries and Food (MAFF), Consultation document, July 1999.

Moore Lappé, F., J. Collins and P. Rosset, *World Hunger: Twelve Myths*, London: Earthscan, 1988.

Murphy, S., *Trade and Food Security. An Assessment of the Uruguay Round Agreement on Agriculture*, London: Catholic Institute for International Relations, 1999.

Overseas Development Institute, *The Debate on GMOs: Relevance for the South*, London: ODI, 1999.

Oxfam, Genetically Modified Crops, *World Trade and Food Security*, Oxford: Oxfam, 1999.

Panagariya, A., 'Seattle: a Failure without Losers', *The Economic Times*, New Delhi, 13 December, 1999.

People's Decade for Human Rights Education, *Human Rights and Economic Globalisation: Directions for the World Trade Organisation*, PDHRE, 1999.

Pretty, J., *Splice*, Vol. 4, No. 6 (August/September 1998).

——, *The Living Land*, London: Earthscan, 1998.

Rosset, P., 'On the Benefits of Small Farms', *Food First Policy Brief*, Vol. 6, No. 4 (Winter, 1999).

Rural Advancement Foundation International, *Plant Breeders' Wrongs*, Ottawa: RAFI, 1999.

'Seeds for the Future', *People & the Planet*, Vol. 8, No. 4 (1999).

Sharma, D., *GATT to WTO: Seeds of Despair*, New Delhi: Konark Publishers, 1995.

——, *Selling Out: the Cost of Free Trade for Food Security in India*, London: UK Food Group, 1999.

Shiva, V. 'The Historic Significance of Seattle', *Splice*, January/February 2000.

Swinbank, A., K. Jordan and N. Beard, *Implications for Developing Countries of Likely Reforms of the Common Agricultural Policy of the European Union*. London: Commonwealth Secretariat, 1999.

'The WTO Aims for Deal with Poorer Nations', *Financial Times*, 14 February 2000.

Thrupp, L. A., with G. Bergeron and W. F. Waters, *Bittersweet Harvests for Global Supermarkets: Challenges in Latin America's Agricultural Export Boom*, Washington: World Resources Institute, 1995.

UK Food Group, *Hungry for Power*, London: UK Food Group, 1999.

United Nations Conference on Trade and Development, *Trade and Development Report*, Geneva: UNCTAD, 1998.

United Nations Development Programme, *Human Development Report 1997*, New York: UNDP, 1997.

——, *Human Development Report*, 1999, New York: UNDP, 1999.

United Nations Environment Programme, *Global Biodiversity Assessment*, UNEP/ Cambridge University Press, 1995.

Vredeseilanden-Coopibo (Ugandan NGO) and others, 'Effects of Agricultural Price and Market Liberalization and Other Factors on Food Security in Selected Districts of Uganda', December 1998.

Warwick, H., 'Cuba's Organic Revolution', *The Ecologist*, Vol. 29, No. 8 (December 1999).

Watkins, K., 'Global Market Myths', *Red Pepper*, June 1996.

World Wildlife Fund, *Learning from Seattle*, WWF–UK Report of the 3rd WTO Ministerial Meeting, December 1999.

RELEVANT ORGANIZATIONS
including websites

Action Aid, Hamlyn House, MacDonald Road, Archway, London N19 5PG. Web: www.actionaid.org

Association of World Council of Churches-related Development Organizations in Europe (APRODEV), Ecumenical Centre, 174 Rue Joseph 11, B-1000 Brussels, Belgium. Web:www.oneworld.org,aprodev

CAFOD, Romero Close, Stockwell Road, London SW9 9TY.
Web: www.cafod.org.uk/cafod

Canadian Centre for Policy Alternatives. Web: www.policyalternatives.ca

Cargill. Web: www/cargill.com

Catholic Institute for International Relations (CIIR), Unit 3, Canonbury Yard, 190a New North Road, London N1 7BJ. Web: www.ciir.org

Centre for Environment and Society, University of Essex, Wivenhoe Park, Colchester CO4 3SQ, UK. Web: www.essex.ac.uk/centres/ces/

Christian Aid, PO Box 100, London SE1 7RT. Web: www.christian-aid.org.uk

CIDSE, Belgium. Web: www. (tba)

Consumers International, 24 Highbury Crescent, London N5 1RX.
Web: www.consumersinternational.org.trade

Corporate Europe Observer. Web:www.xs4all.nl

Department for International Development (DFID). Web: www.dfid.gov.uk

European Commission. Web: http://europa/int.comm/trade,
Web: http://europa/int.comm/agriculture

European Fair Trade Association. 7a rue E.Michiels, B-1080, Brussels, Belgium.
E-mail:eftaadocacy@Compuserve.com

European Research Office, Grasmarkt 105 bus 46 – 1000 Brussels.
E-mail: bnero@village.uunet.be

Eurostep, 115 Rue Stevin, 1000 Brussels, Belgium. Web: www.oneworld.org/eurostep

Fairtrade Foundation, Suite 204, 16 Baldwin's Gardens, London EC1N 7RJ.
Web: www.fairtrade.org.uk

Food and Agriculture Organization (FAO), Viale delle Terme di Caracalla, 00100, Rome, Italy. Web:www.fao.org

Focus on Global South, c/o CUSRI, Chulalongkorn University, Bangkok 10330, Thailand. Web: www.focusweb.org

Friends of the Earth, 26-28 Underwood Street, London N1 7JQ. Web:www.foe.co.uk

Greenpeace, Keizersgracht 176, 1016 DW Amsterdam, The Netherlands.
Web: www.greenpeace.org

Institute for Agriculture and Trade Policy, 2105 First Avenue South, Minneapolis, MN 55404-2505, US. Web: www.iatp.org/

Liaison Committee of Development NGOs to the EU. Web: www. oneworld.org/liaison

New Economics Foundation, 6-8 Cole Street, London SE1 4YH.
Web: www.neweconomics.org

Organization of African Unity, PO Box 3243, Addis Ababa, Ethiopia. Fax: (251-1) 512622.

Oxfam, GB, 274, Banbury Road, Oxford, OX2 7DZ. Web: www.oxfam.org.uk

Permaculture Association, UK. Web: www.permaculture.org.uk

People's Decade for Human Rights Education, Eurolink Business Centre, Suite 13. London SW2 1BZ. Web: www.pdhre.org

People for Fair Trade. Web: www.peopleforfairtrade.org

Rural Advancement Foundation International (RAFI), Canada, Web: www.rafi.org

South Centre, Ch. du Champ d'Anier 17, 1211 Geneva 19, Switzerland.
Web: www.southcentre.org

The International Coalition for Development Action (ICDA). Web: www.icda.be - issues regular 'Impact Lists' about WTO matters.

The One World website - www.oneworld.org - also includes organizations working on food and trade issues.

Third World Network: 228 Macalister Street, 10400 Penang, Malaysia.
Web: www.twnside.org.sg

Third World Network, Africa Secretariat, PO Box AN19452, Accra, Ghana.
E-mail: isodec@ghana.com

Trans-Atlantic Business Dialogue. Web: www.tabd.org

UK Food Group, PO Box 100, London SE1 7RT. Web: www.ukfg.org.uk

United Nations Conference on Trade and Development (UNCTAD), Palais des Nations, 1211 Geneva, Switzerland. Web:www.unctad.org

UNICE, Rue Joseph 11, 40/4 - B-1000 Brussels, Belgium. Web: www.unice.org

Vannoppen, Jan, Vredeseilanden-Coopibo;
E-mail: jan.vannoppen@vredeseilanden-coopibo.ngonet.be

Via Campesina. E-mail: viacam@gbm.hn

World Health Organization (WHO), 1211, Geneva 27, Switzerland. Web: www.who.ch

World Wildlife Fund (WWF), CH-1196 Gland, Switzerland. Web: www.panda.org

World Development Movement, 25 Beehive Place, London SW9 7QR.
Web: www.wdm.org.uk

World Economic Forum. Web: www.weforum.org

World Trade Organization (WTO), Rue de Lausanne, Geneva, Switzerland.
Web: www.wto.org

NOTES

Chapter 1

1 The AIE papers were officially classed as 'non-papers'. They were not formally published and there are no references for them.

2 Statement of the African Trade Network, November 1999.

3 Speech to EU trade ministers, Florence, Italy, October 1999.

4 Conversation with author, December 1999.

5 'Future ACP Trade', *The Courier,* October/November 1999, Brussels, European Commission

6 Speech to NGO meeting in Seattle, December 1999.

7 Conversation with author, November 1999.

8 'Big Business Voice Drowns Cries of Street Protesters', Christian Aid press release and conversation with author, 30 November 1999.

9 Media release, Corporate Europe Observatory, 3 December 1999.

10 Conversation with author, 2 December 1999.

11 WTO Press Release, No. 156, 'Seattle Conference Doomed to Succeed, Says Moore', 30 November 1999.

12 Conversation with author, December 1999.

13 Joint communique (Latin American and Caribbean countries), 2 December 1999.

14 Organization of African Unity communique, 2 December 1999.

15 *Learning from Seattle*, WWF-UK Report of the Third WTO Ministerial Meeting, December 1999.

16 Draft of the chairman of the Seattle Ministerial meeting working group on agriculture, 2 December 1999.

17 *Ibid.*

18 UK Food Group position paper on Seattle, November 1999.

19 'Brussels Blind Spot', APRODEV, October 1999.

20 Conversation with author, December 1999.

21 A. Panagariya, 'Seattle: a Failure without Losers', *The Economic Times,* New Delhi, 13 December 1999.

22 Devinder Sharma, *The Fiasco at Seattle,* International Coalition for Development Action website, 23 December 1999.

23 Conversations with author, December 1999, at the conclusion of the Seattle meeting.
24 Remarks of Charlene Barshefsky, Closing Plenary Session, 3 December 1999.
25 Conversation with author, December 1999.
26 Martin Khor, *International Herald Tribune,* 21 December 1999.
27 *Ibid.*
28 Press release, 4 December 1999.
29 Sharma, *The Fiasco at Seattle.*
30 Barry Coates, director of the World Development Movement, conversation with author, December 1999.
31 Sharma, *The Fiasco at Seattle.*
32 Scott Sinclair, Canadian Centre for Policy Alternatives, e-mail, 17 January 2000.
33 Vandana Shiva, 'The Historic Significance of Seattle', *Splice,* January/February 2000.
34 'The WTO Aims for Deal with Poorer Nations', *Financial Times,* 14 February 2000.

Chapter 2

1 José Muchnik, food researcher, quoted in *Spore,* No. 83 (October 1999), Wageningen: Technical Centre for Agricultural and Rural Cooperation (CTA) (ACP–EU).
2 M. S. Swaminathan, BBC World Service, *One Planet,* 5 January 2000.
3 Paper prepared for an Inter-Parliamentary Conference, Rome: FAO, 29 November –2 December 1998.
4 'The State of Food Insecurity in the World 1999', Rome: FAO, 1999.
5 Africa Watch, *Africa Recovery,* New York: United Nations, 1998.
6 Jules Pretty, BBC World Service, *One Planet,* 5 January 2000.
7 *Agriculture: Towards 2010,* Rome: FAO, 1993, pp. 276–7.
8 *Nutrient Depletion in the Agricultural Soils of Africa,* International Food Policy Research Institute, Washington: 1999.
9 Susanna Davies, *Adaptable Livelihoods, Coping with Food Insecurity in the Malian Sahel,* Basingstoke: MacMillan, 1996.
10 Speech, October 1999, to a consultation on rural women and information.
11 *World Disasters Report,* International Federation of Red Cross and Red Crescent Societies/OUP, Oxford, 1999.
12 *Human Development Report 1997,* New York: United Nations Development Programme.
13 *World Disasters Report,* International Federation of Red Cross and Red Crescent Societies/OUP, Oxford, 1996.
14 See *International Agricultural Development* magazine, July/August 1998.
15 See Roger Blench, *Seasonal Climatic Forecasting,* London: ODI, November 1999.
16 D. Hinrichsen and J. Rowley, 'A Look into the Future World of 8 Billion Humans', *People & the Planet,* Vol. 8, No. 4 (1999).
17 *Peoples, Plants and Patents,* The Crucible Group. Canada: International Development Research Centre, 1994.

18 *Global Biodiversity Assessment*, United Nations Environment Programme/ Cambridge University Press, November 1995.
19 Speech to Convention on Biological Diversity conference, December 1994.

Chapter 3

1 Susan George, *The Lugano Report*, London: Pluto Press, 1999, p. 105.
2 *Food and International Trade*, Rome: FAO, 1996.
3 *Ibid*.
4 Sophia Murphy, *Trade and Food Security. An Assessment of the Uruguay Round Agreement on Agriculture*, London: CIIR, 1999, p. 45.
5 Speech to a meeting at the Royal Commonwealth Society, London, 14 October 1999.
6 Maurizio Bussolo and Henri-Bernard Solignac Lecomte, *Trade Liberalisation and Poverty*, Overseas Development Institute, 1999.
7 View expressed to a meeting at the Royal Commonwealth Society, London, 14 October 1999.
8 Comment to aid agency worker, October 1999.
9 Speech to a meeting at the Royal Commonwealth Society, London, 14 October 1999.
10 Harold James, 'Is Liberalization Reversible?', *Finance & Development,* December 1999, Washington: IMF.
11 Bussolo and Solignac Lecomte, *Trade Liberalisation and Poverty*.
12 M. S. Swaminathan, BBC World Service, *One Planet* , 5 January 2000.
13 Kevin Bundell and Eileen Maybin, *After the Prawn Rush*, London: Christian Aid, 1996.
14 'Bean Counting in Chile', *The World Paper,* Boston: December 1993.
15 L. A. Thrupp, with G. Bergeron and W. F. Waters, *Bittersweet Harvests for Global Supermarkets: Challenges in Latin America's Agricultural Export Boom*, Washington: World Resources Institute, 1995.
16 Conversation with author, May 1994.

Chapter 4

1 Conversation with author, February 1998.
2 Speech to a meeting at the Royal Institute of International Affairs, London, 16 January 1998.
3 Jack Kemp, former US Congressman, 'Third Way Route Jams Trade', *Financial Times*, 2 August 1999.
4 Statement to the Second WTO Ministerial Meeting, May 1998.
5 WTO website, '"Glossary of Terms": An Informal Press Guide to "WTO Speak"'.
6 Communication to author, July 1999.
7 Ministry of Agriculture, Fisheries and Food, consultation document, July 1999.

8   Myriam van der Stichele, speech to NGO meeting in Geneva, May 1998.

9   K. Watkins, 'Global Market Myths', *Red Pepper,* June 1996, p. 14.

10 World Development Movement paper on regulation, London, 1999.

11 Conversation with author, February 1998.

12 *Human Rights and Economic Globalisation: Directions for the World Trade Organisation,* PDHRE, 1999.

13 Sharma, *The Fiasco at Seattle.*

14 Conversation with author, 2 December 1999.

15 Amy L. Kazmin, 'WTO Chief Urges India to Back New Trade Talks', *Financial Times,* 11 January 2000.

16 *Trade and Development Report,* Geneva: UNCTAD, 1998.

17 'Meeting Needs of Developing Countries', *Financial Times,* 12 August 1999.

18 UNCTAD Press Release, TAD/INF/2812, 5 July 1999.

19 Focus on Trade newsletter, Bangkok: January 2000.

20 Action Aid, e-mail to author, 18 February 2000.

21 'The MFCAL Concept', paper prepared for Maastricht conference on 'The Multifunctional Character of Agriculture and Land', Rome: FAO, September 1999.

22 Statement, FAO website, July 1999.

23 *Ibid.*

24 *Human Development Report, 1999,* New York: UNDP, 1999.

25 Alan Swinbank, Kate Jordan and Nick Beard, *Implications for Developing Countries of Likely Reforms of the Common Agricultural Policy of the European Union.* London: Commonwealth Secretariat, 1999.

26 'WTO's New Chief Goes into Battle to Defend Free Trade', *The Independent,* 7 September 1999.

27 Speech to EuronAid/EU-NGDO conference, 'Agenda 2000, CAP Reform and Global Food Security', Madrid, November 1998.

28 Murphy, *Trade and Food Security.*

Chapter 5

1   FAO Symposium on Agriculture, Trade and Food Security, Geneva, 23–24 September 1999, Synthesis of Case Studies, X3065/E, Rome: FAO, September 1999.

2   Conversation with author, September 1999.

3   John Madeley (ed.), *Trade and the Hungry: How International Trade Is Causing Hunger.* Brussels: APRODEV, 1999.

4   This section is based on Devinder Sharma, *Selling Out: the Cost of Free Trade for Food Security in India,* London: UK Food Group, 1999, and on interviews with Vandana Shiva (October 1999) and Devinder Sharma (November 1999.)

5   Interviewed by the author in Seattle, December 1999.

6   M. Chisvo, *Trade Liberalisation and Household Food Security: a Study from Zimbabwe,* London: CIIR, March 2000.

7   Adapted from a Friends of the Earth, Uruguay case study, 1999.

8   Adapted from Sharma, *Selling Out.*

9   M. Lundberg and B. Milanovic, 'The Truth about Global Inequality', *Financial*

Times, 25 February 2000.

10 See, for example, speech by Clare Short, Britain's International Development Secretary, 3 November 1999, 'Making the Next Round Work for the World's Poor'.

Chapter 6

1 J. Madeley, *Big Business, Poor Peoples*, London: Zed Books, 1999.

2 See Cargill's website.

3 B. Kneen, *Invisible Giant*, London: Pluto Press, 1996.

4 B. Kneen, chapter in *Hungry for Power*, London: UK Food Group, 1999.

5 *Ibid.*

6 K. Watkins, 'Global Market Myths', *Red Pepper*, June 1996.

7 Ralph Nader, interview with author, December 1999.

8 G. Monbiot, *The Guardian*, 16 December 1999.

9 See M. A. Altieri and P. Rosset, 'Ten Reasons Why Biotechnology Will Not Ensure Food Security, Protect the Environment and Reduce Poverty in the Developing World', paper presented to an NGO meeting in Seattle, December 1999.

10 Mark Curtis, Action Aid, press release, November 1999.

11 *Crops and Robbers: Biopiracy and the Patenting of Staple Food Crops*, London: Action Aid, November 1999.

12 *Patenting of Life, the Poor and Food Security*, Brussels: CIDSE, 1999.

13 Corporate Europe Observer website.

14. *TRIPs and Farmers' Rights*, London: Action Aid, November 1999.

15 Philomenon Yang, Cameroon Ambassador, speech on behalf of the African group to UN Convention on Biodiversity, July 1999.

16 Quoted in *International Agricultural Development* magazine, September/October 1993.

17 *Patenting of Life*.

18 'Biodiversity in Agriculture: Policy Issues'. *ILEIA Newsletter*, Leusden, the Netherlands, December 1999.

19 Statement by representatives of indigenous peoples, Seattle, December 1999.

20 RAFI occasional paper, Vol. 1, No. 1, Ottawa: RAFI, 1994.

21 'Plant Breeders' Wrongs', Ottawa: RAFI, 1999.

22 *Crops and Robbers*.

23 RAFI website 1999.

24 Speech to the Board of Directors of Monsanto, June 1999.

25 *Patenting of Life*.

26 *Crops and Robbers*.

27 'Biodiversity in Agriculture', op. cit.

28 Devinder Sharma, *GATT to WTO: Seeds of Despair*, New Delhi: Konark Publishers, 1995.

29 Pradeep Mehta, statement, 24 December 1999.

30 *Crops and Robbers*.

Chapter 7

1 US Department of Agriculture report, 1999, quoted in Altieri and Rosset, 'Ten Reasons'.

2 Communication to Gaia Foundation, May 1998.

3 Liz Hosken, Gaia Foundation, communication to author, August 1999.

4 *The Debate on GMOs: Relevance for the South*, London: ODI, 1999.

5 Statement, June 1998.

6 *Ibid*.

7 RAFI website, 1999.

8 Letter of Robert Shapiro to Gordon Conway, Rockefeller Foundation, 4 October 1999.

9 RAFI website, 1999.

10 Letter of Robert Shapiro.

11 *Ibid*.

12 Conversation with author, December 1999.

13 RAFI website, 1999.

14 'RAFI Communique', February/March 2000.

15 *Genetically Modified Crops, World Trade and Food Security*, Oxford: Oxfam GB, 1999.

16 Jules Pretty, *Splice,* August/September 1998.

17 Michael Lipton, speech to Worldaware meeting, London, 9 December 1999.

18 World Health Organization website.

19 *Genetically Modified Crops*, op. cit.

20 Vandana Shiva, letter to Oxfam, 4 November 1999.

21 *Genetically Modified Crops*, op. cit.

22 Conversation with author, December 1999.

23 Speech to NGO meeting in Seattle, 2 December 1999.

24 'America Backs Down on GM foods', *The Observer,* 30 January 2000.

25 E-mail to author from Clare Joy, World Development Movement, 28 January 2000.

26 Communication to author, January 2000.

27 Department of the UK Environment, Transport and the Regions, press release, 29 January 2000.

28 E-mail to author from Clare Joy.

Chapter 8

1 *Putting Food Security into the World Trade Organisation*, Brussels: Liaison Committee of Development NGOs to the EU, 1999.

2 Statement by Friends of the Earth, UK, December 1999.

3 'Take Agriculture out of WTO', statement by Via Campesina, 3 December 1999.

4 Statement, December 1999.

5 Peter Rosset, Food First, speech to NGO meeting in Seattle, December 1999.

6 CAFOD, House of Lords submission on the WTO, February 2000.

7 UK Food Group, Memorandum to the International Development Select

Committee of the House of Commons, February 2000.

8 Claire Melamed, Christian Aid, correspondence with author, March 2000.

9 Adapted from Focus on Trade newsletter, No. 43 (January 2000), Bangkok.

Chapter 9

1 Quoted in 'Seeds for the Future', *People & the Planet* magazine, Vol. 8, No. 4 (1999).

2 Jules Pretty, BBC World Service, *One Planet*, 5 January 2000.

3 *Ibid.*

4 Quoted in 'Seeds for the Future'.

5 Conversation with author, June 1999. See *International Agricultural Development* magazine, November/December 1999, for further examples of higher yields from agriculture with low external inputs.

6 I interviewed Bill Mollison in October 1991 at the Permaculture Institute (PO Box 1, Tyalgum, NSW, Australia). Nine years later, Mollison's comments strike a prophetic note.

7 See *International Agricultural Development* magazine, May/June 1994.

8 Conversation with author, November 1996.

9 *Ibid.*

10 P. Rosset, 'On the Benefits of Small Farms', *Food First Policy Brief*, Vol. 6, No. 4 (Winter 1999).

11 H. Warwick, 'Cuba's Organic Revolution', *The Ecologist*, Vol 29, No 8, December 1999, pp. 457–460.

12 Quoted in Warwick, 'Cuba's Organic Revolution'.

13 Conversation with author, December 1999.

14 Jan Vannoppen, *Participatory Research on Market Liberalisation and Food Security in Uganda*, Vredeseilanden-Coopibo: February 2000.

15 Conversation with author, February 1999.

INDEX

Abu, John 17

accountability 24, 140-1

Action Aid 82, 101, 104

Addis Ababa 116

Africa, climate change threatens famine in 28; and colonialism 42; EU dumping in 71; flower exports of 55; and food security 144, 154; and genetically modified foods 107; hunger in 154; and industrialization of food 14; NGOs and 75; North 26, 31; and patents on plants 94; at Seattle 17, 21-2, 24, 65, 81; soil depletion in 30; Southern 40, 71, 93; sub-Saharan 26, 32, 34, 37-8, 40, 48, 71; West 31, 40; and Western science 107; women farmers in 32; and WTO 10-11, *see also* at Seattle

African, Caribbean and Pacific countries (ACP) 14, 61

Agenda 2000 69

agriculture, agribusiness 37-8, 78; biodiversity in 39, 126, 131, 137; cash-crop 86, 132, 152; climate change and 36; community organization in, 144; conflict and 35; corporate 4-5, 79, 88; dumping weakens 70-3, 76-7, 80, 122; ecological 112, 126, 144; and economic growth 47-8; employment in 13, 26, 29, 67, 79, 81; and the environment 26, 67, 112, 126, 144; ethics of 146; export 1, 18, 30, 43, 53-5, 68, 76-7, 79, 83, 92, 132, 137; extension services 85-6; family 87, 126, 131; floriculture 54-6, 88-9; and food security 36, 51, -7; food-crop 76-7; under GATT 44; and genetically modified foods 117-20, 127; and globalization 3, 94, 119; green revolution and 29; high-yield crops 38; HIV/Aids and 38, 40; indigenous 125; industrialization of 14, 26, 48, 83, 103, 143; input costs 28, 51, 77-8, 84, 86, 89, 112, 117, 146; input subsidies 61; investment in 86, 125; land distribution and 87, 133, 135; with

low external inputs 5-6, 150; with low-cost technologies 144; management of 112, 120; marginalization of 29, 54-5, 123; market gardens 86; and markets 29, 32, 48, 86, 132; monocultural 5, 38, 94, 120; multifunctional 9, 13, 26, 126; natural disasters and 33, 45; 'New Deal' for 67; organic 6, 117, 119, 143, 146-7, 150-2, permaculture 6, 145-7, 154; and poverty 29, -7; productivity in 48, 75, 112, 117, 124, 144-5, 151; protection of 14, 45, 63, 85, 87, 125; research on 33, 55, 87; and rural economies 13; sea-level rises and 36-7; small 3-5, 29, 37-8, 70, 73, 75-9, 81-2, 85-7, 92, 106, 108, 110-12, 115, 123, 125-6, 137, 150-2; in small countries 9; soil erosion and 146-7; soil infertility and 30; state support for 8, 18, 44-5, 58-9, 61, 69-70, 74, 76, 79, 84-6, 92; subsidization of 13-14, 17-19, 58, 69-70, 79, 84-6, 122, 125-6, 132, 138; subsistence 8, 37-8, 103; sustainable 51, 88, 107, 112, 122, 126, 144-5; and technology 29; TNCs and 3, 37-8, 91, 94-6; trade liberalization and 24, 44, 46, 48, 52, 56, 122, 128; traditional knowledge of 6, 134; TRIMS and 47; TRIPs and 46; UNCTAD and 67; underfunded 2, 29, 33; urban 152; US and EU fail to agree on 22; water-harvesting techniques in 144, 146; women and 2, 32-3, 77, 86; world model of 83; WTO and 24, 122, 130, 132; *see also* seeds; WTO, Agreement on Agriculture

aid 3, 18, 34, 44-5, 53, 57, 69, 123-4, 147

Algeria 31

Altieri, Miguel 117-20

analysis and information exchange (AIE) 8-9

Andhra Pradesh state 78, 88

apartheid 12

apples 88

aquaculture 53

Participating Organizations

- **Both ENDS:** A service and advocacy organization which collaborates with environment and indigenous organizations, both in the South and in the North, with the aim of helping to create and sustain a vigilant and effective environmental movement.
  Email: info@bothends.org   *Website:* www.bothends.org

- **Catholic Institute for International Relations (CIIR):** CIIR aims to contribute to the eradication of poverty through a programme that combines advocacy at national and international level with community-based development.
  Email: ciir@ciir.org   *Website:* www.ciir.org

- **Corner House:** The Corner House is a UK-based research and solidarity group working on social and environmental justice issues in North and South.
  Email: cornerhouse@gn.apc.org   *Website:* www.cornerhouse.icaap.org

- **Focus on the Global South:** Focus is dedicated to regional and global policy analysis and advocacy work. It works to strengthen the capacity of organizations of the poor and marginalized people of the South and to better analyse and understand the impacts of the globalization process on their daily lives.
  Email: Admin@focusweb.org   *Website:* www.focusweb.org

- **Inter Pares:** Inter Pares, a Canadian social justice organization, has been active since 1975 in building relationships with Third World development groups and providing support for community-based development programs. Inter Pares is also involved in education and advocacy in Canada, promoting understanding about the causes, effects and solutions to poverty.
  58 rue Arthur Street, Ottawa, Ontario, K1R 7B9 Canada
  Phone: + 1 (613) 563-4801   *Fax:* + 1 (613) 594-4704

- **Third World Network:** TWN is an international network of groups and individuals involved in efforts to bring about a greater articulation of the needs and rights of peoples in the Third World; a fair distribution of the world's resources; and forms of development which are ecologically sustainable and fulfil human needs. Its international secretariat is based in Penang, Malaysia.
  Email: twnet@po.jaring.my   *Website:* www.twnside.org.sg

- **World Development Movement (WDM):** The World Development Movement campaigns to tackle the causes of poverty and injustice. It is a democratic membership movement that works with partners in the South to cancel unpayable debt and break the ties of IMF conditionality, for fairer trade and investment rules, and for strong international rules on multinationals.
  E-mail: wdm@wdm.org.uk   *Website:* www.wdm.org.uk

THIS BOOK IS AVAILABLE IN THE FOLLOWING COUNTRIES:

FIJI
University Book Centre
University of South Pacific
Suva

Tel: 679 313 900
Fax: 679 303 265

GHANA
EPP Book Services
PO Box TF 490
Trade Fair
Accra

Tel: 233 21 773087
Fax: 233 21 779099

INDIA
Segment Book Distributors
B-23/25 Kailash Colony
New Delhi

Tel: 91 11 644 3013
Fax: 91 11 647 0472

MOZAMBIQUE
Sul Sensacoes
PO Box 2242
Maputo

Tel: 258 1 421 974
Fax: 258 1 423 414

NEPAL
Everest Media Services
GPO Box 5443, Dillibazar
Putalisadak Chowk
Kathmandu

Tel: 977 1 416 026
Fax: 977 1 250 176

PAPUA NEW GUINEA
Unisearch PNG Pty Ltd
Box 320, University
National Capital District

Tel: 675 326 0130
Fax: 675 326 0127

RWANDA
Librairie Ikirezi
PO Box 443,
Kigali

Tel/fax: 250 71314

TANZANIA
TEMA Publishing Co Ltd
PO Box 63115
Dar es Salaam

Tel: 255 51 113608
Fax: 255 51 110472

ZAMBIA
UNZA Press
University of Zambia
PO Box 32379
Lusaka

Tel: 260 1 290 409
Fax: 260 1 253 952